Designing Staircases

WILLIBALD MANNES

VNR **VAN NOSTRAND REINHOLD COMPANY**
NEW YORK CINCINNATI TORONTO LONDON MELBOURNE

Willibald Mannes was born in 1925. A master carpenter and architect in private practice, he is also the proprietor of a concern which specializes in staircase construction. He sits on German and international standards committees and is the author of numerous articles published in specialist journals. His book *Treppen und Geländer* ("Staircases and Balustrades") was published in 1971 and a number of individual entries from it form part of this book.

Translation copyright © 1982 by Van Nostrand Reinhold Company Inc.
Originally published in Germany under the title GESTALTETE TREPPEN
by Deutsche Verlags – Anstalt Gmbh
© 1974 Deutsche Verlags – Anstalt Gmbh
Neckarstrasse 121, 2000 Stuttgart 1

Library of Congress Catalog Card Number 80-21145
ISBN 0-442-22578-4

Printed in the United States of America

Published by Van Nostrand Reinhold Company Inc.
135 West 50th Street
New York, NY 10020

Van Nostrand Reinhold Limited
1410 Birchmount Road
Scarborough, Ontario M1P 2E7, Canada

Van Nostrand Reinhold Australia Pty. Ltd.
17 Queen Street
Mitcham, Victoria 3132, Australia

Van Nostrand Reinhold Company Limited
Molly Millars Lane
Wokingham, Berkshire, England

16 15 14 13 12 11 10 9 8 7 6 5 4 3 2 1

Library of Congress Cataloging in Publication Data

Mannes, Willibald, 1925–
    Designing staircases.

    Translation of Gestaltete Treppen.
    Includes indexes.
    1. Staircases. 2. Stairs. I. Title.
NA3060.M3413   721'.832   80-21145
ISBN 0-442-22578-4

Contents

3

Foreword

The role of the staircase within a building is that of connecting different levels in the shortest and yet the most convenient way possible. However, in negotiating the slopes that arise between vertical and horizontal surfaces, a staircase is often forced to change direction, thus creating curves, twisted surfaces, and spiraled forms; no other part of the construction process has the possibility for such a variety of forms, such potential for real "design."

Fine examples of the art of staircase building are to be found in every period throughout the history of building construction. In our own age, though functional design dominates, a handful of craftsmen are attempting to reverse the trend by producing highly individual work. As an architect and a craftsman, I try to equate my design ideas with what is possible under today's conditions and to achieve it by working in conjunction with my trusted team of craftsmen. The majority of the staircases we have designed and built are to be found in the picture section of this book.

No doubt much criticism can and will be leveled on the grounds of modern sensitivity and those staircases described as stylized cannot be compared with the more traditional and classic versions. There is much compromise and much that is far from complete, but, nevertheless, the numerous examples illustrated should serve as an inspiration for experimental and innovative design.

The picture section, which occupies the major part of this book, is preceded by a short theoretical section, and the general techniques of staircase construction are summed up concisely and illustrated with sketches and many staircases are drawn in great detail. I also touch on new construction techniques and deal with safety standards and regulations. This book attempts to live up to its title, *Designing Staircases,* and also to summarize the wide area of staircase construction in general and wooden staircases in particular. I hope that I have made accessible and familiar those aspects of the subject that architects, contractors, and those engaged in staircase construction will find relevant to their own area of operation.

Willibald Mannes

1 Materials

1.1 Wood

Despite the development and application of new materials, wood still holds its own as one of the traditional materials used in staircase construction. Two factors make it ideal for this use: its versatility and the living color and structure of the grain. These allow it to fulfill both practical and aesthetic considerations.

The abrasion resistance of each wood varies from one type to another, but basically, all the types of wood described on pages 10 and 11 are suitable for use in any part of the staircase. However, it should be borne in mind that soft woods are not recommended for treads that will be subject to heavy traffic. For this reason, the summary of common wood types used in staircase building that follows is divided into soft and hard woods. In order to protect hard woods from premature abrasion and to avoid damage to the surface of the wood, all surfaces should be sealed.

The use of wood in staircase construction has significant static advantages, which lie mainly in its high resistance to stress caused by bending. Naturally, this varies from wood to wood. Thus 2.0-cm boards are suitable for use in a standard domestic staircase of treads up to widths of one meter and 2.7 cm for treads of above one meter and up to one meter 22 cm, the maximum width; even strings and bearing beams can be kept relatively thin because of this property.

The shrinkage of wood used in staircase construction is approximately 10–12%. In extreme cases, wood will shrink a further 6–8% when installed (for example above radiators). If this is to be the case, the wood to be used should be predried artificially by a further 8–10%. In the case of particularly expensive staircases, laminated timber should be chosen as a material (e.g., plywood, blockboard, chipboard) to provide a ligature against warping that might occur later.

Wooden stairs can have an extremely long lifespan if certain important ground rules are observed, namely that the use of certain very soft or worm-prone woods should be avoided, e.g., poplar, alder, or linden. Stone pine, for instance, is only suitable as a veneer. Oak, pine, or larch should be chosen when the staircase is going to be situated in a humid or damp area and, in Europe, non-European woods should be used only with care. However, the non-European woods described below have been well tried and can be used without hesitation. Timber waste in these types of wood varies considerably; it is much greater in the case of oak than in pines, since the degree of sapwood in oak can frequently amount to 20–25%, and this cannot be used. Timber waste must, therefore, be taken into account when calculating how much wood is required or when purchasing stocks.

1.1.1 Treatment of wood surfaces

1.1.1.1 Pretreatment of oak
1.1.1.1.1 Darkened (fumed) oak
Ready staircase sections are stored in hermetically sealed chambers in which liquid ammonia is placed in flat containers. The ammoniac fumes penetrate into the surface of the wood and give it color. The length of time the wood should be thus stored depends on the depth of color desired. When exposed to ammonia fumes for six to seven days, a depth of 5–8 mm is obtained. For treads, strings, and other parts of staircases, a penetration of 2–3 mm is desirable (i.e., about three days exposure to the fumes). Timber treated in this way must be left in the open air for about two days before further work can be carried out on its surface. This darkening process produces a warm, tobacco-brown color.

1.1.1.1.2 Lime-washed oak
This process is only suitable for larger surfaces, such as strings, risers, and infill panels. The surface pores are brushed clean or, if possible, blasted clean with compressed air. In order to prevent the pores from absorbing too much of the filler, the surfaces should be treated with a light-filtering substance before the lime-washing takes place. The filler, made of white powder mixed with pore liquid, should be rubbed vigorously into the pores across the grain of the wood, using a rough linen cloth. Surfaces treated in this way can then be sprayed with a very thin clear or mat varnish when dry.

1.1.1.1.3 Stained and lime-washed oak
This combination of processes results in a particularly attractive surface appearance, highlighting the color contrast between the dark patches and the lighter pores to maximum effect.

1.1.1.2 Treating the surfaces of various woods
1.1.1.2.1 Staining
The tone that is eventually achieved in staining always depends on the properties of the wood used (basic color, how hard it is, and how absorbent it proves to be). In woods that contain tannin, the level of tannin content plays a significant role, since it affects the chemicals in the stain in various ways. The stain depth and color obtained will also be influenced greatly by the method of application, and, naturally, the longer the stain is left to soak into the wood, the darker and richer the color produced will be. Of course, every stain looks different on a veneer from what it looks like on solid wood.

Since it is rare for very large surfaces to be involved in staircase construction, simple staining processes, such as those that are water-, spirit-, or ammonia-based, are usually adequate. Stains are most suitable for woods where soft and hard growth rings are present, giving an even coloring to the dark (hard) and light (soft) rings. Stains that have recently come onto the market which are specifically designed to give a rustic effect are particularly interesting.

1.1.1.2.2 Bleaching

Surfaces that have already been plastered can be treated with hydrogen peroxide or other bleaching agents. After drying, any surplus salts remaining on the surface should be removed, using warm water, before the surface is treated further. Woods bleached with hydrogen peroxide should not be treated with DD varnishes, since the remains of the bleach will cause a strong orange-yellow discoloration.

1.1.1.3 Colorless coatings for timber surfaces

It is a basic rule that all timber surfaces should be treated before the staircase is installed. This can be done when the sections are still in the workshop, since the temperature there approximates the room temperature in the stairwell.

Coating mediums that can be sprayed on easily or applied with a brush are recommended. In the case of light woods, varnishes with a filter against ultraviolet light should be used to delay darkening or yellowing. Each further layer of applied colorless coating will give the surface a harder and more resistant finish. The choice of the medium to be used depends on the amount of stress and strain to which the surface will be subject and on the type of polished finish required.

1.1.1.3.1 Sealing

In sealing, the combined effect of two ingredients—varnish and hardener—is to provide a fabric-like surface that retains its elasticity and flexibility even when set dry. For example, a sheet of paper that has been sealed can be folded sharply without damage to the sealant at the edges of the fold; whereas, if normal varnish were to be used, it would crack and crumble along the fold line.

Innovations in sealing processes over the last few years have brought wooden treads back into favor. Two fundamentally different methods are in common use. The first of these is sealing by impregnation, where the sealant penetrates the surface of the wood and toughens it from within; this method of treatment is not advisable for surfaces that will be subject to heavy traffic (e.g., risers). The second method is to apply a film sealant, which acts as a mat or shiny layer on the wood's surface, so that the wood itself is not touched when in service and the covering protective layer prevents it from wearing one. Stairs that are in constant use should be sealed twice before installation and resealed once or twice at intervals of about three years.

Lime or cement splashes leave dark marks that penetrate deeply into untreated wood and are visable even on primed wood. However, lime, cement, or gypsum mortar leave no traces on mat varnished or sealed surfaces. It should be noted that it is much easier, and more effective, to paint or spray the various surfaces in the workshop before the staircase is assembled.

Installation without prior treatment of surfaces is not advisable, since damp tends to penetrate right to the heart of the wood and later, once the wood has dried out, this can give rise to unpleasant creaking sounds. A further problem is created by the possibility of water, lime, or cement splashes on untreated surfaces, leaving behind unsightly dark patches that are difficult to remove. For these reasons, all parts of the staircase should be surface-treated before installation.

1.1.1.3.2 Varnishing

Varnishing is cheaper than sealing. A shiny or mat effect can be obtained almost equally well by either process, but with varying degrees of durability.

1.1.1.3.3 Mat varnishing

Mat varnish forms a relatively thin surface layer in contrast to gloss varnish and it should be sprayed on. However, a mat surface retains the character of natural wood better than does a sealed or gloss-varnished one.

Coating of cement, gypsum, and lime mortars

Varnished surface

Mat-varnished surface

Primed surface

Untreated surface

Coating of cement, gypsum, and lime mortars rinsed off

Varnished surface

Mat-varnished surface

Primed surface

Untreated surface

Cement   Gypsum   Lime

1.1.2 Solid timber

1.1.2.1 Solid timber—structure
Plain sawn timber (1) cups laterally in a marked fashion and the surface becomes distorted. (2) shows the direction of the growth rings. (3) is defined as the right, (4) as the left side.

After cupping, the degree of warping, depending on the type of wood, is usually 6–10% in the direction of the growth rings (5) and 2–5% vertical to the rings (6). Longitudinally, solid wood will warp approximately 0.1–0.5%.

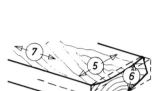

Quarter-sawn timber with this formation of rings distorts hardly at all and cups very little laterally. This cut must be used when high-quality work is demanded.

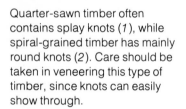

Quarter-sawn timber often contains splay knots (1), while spiral-grained timber has mainly round knots (2). Care should be taken in veneering this type of timber, since knots can easily show through.

1.1.2.2 Bonding solid timber
Bonded timbers are to be highly recommended. Gluing the timbers flat is only possible with soft wood; in hard wood, surfaces to be glued should first be roughened with a toothed plane (1), or a joint seal should be used, or, alternatively, dowels should be sunk.

Laminated timbers where internal spline joints are used are far more resistant to stress. The splines (1) are made from cross-grained wood or plywood and are notched. This method of bonding is, however, time-consuming.

Good longitudinal joints are created by using the tongue-and-groove method. By joggling the wood in a tooth-shaped pattern, almost twice the amount of surface area is created to take the adhesive.

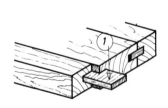

This type of bonding runs across the grain. A finger-joint like this is so durable, that, if tested for resistance to stress, the break will occur alongside the glued section rather than along the joint.

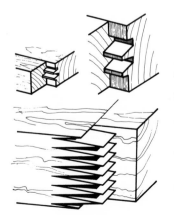

1.2 Various materials

1.2.1 Plywood and chipboard

Plywood is the collective term for veneer board, blockboard and laminboard.

Plywood (veneer board) can consist of three, five, seven, or any uneven number of laminae which cross each other in the direction of the grain. Usual thicknesses (1) are: 4, 5, 6, 8, 10, 12, 15 and 20 mm.

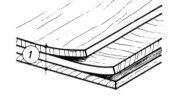

Blockboard consists of core strips (1), which are approximately 2.5–3 cm thick and usually of spruce, pine, poplar or non-European soft woods, placed in alternate grain directions. A layer of veneer (up to 3.7 mm thick) is adhered across these (2). Thicknesses are: 13, 16, 19, 22, 25, 28, 32, 38, and 45 mm.

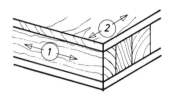

Laminboard has the same properties and advantages as blockboard and is held flat by its narrow core strips.

Platen-pressed chipboard, a three-layer board consisting of wood or flax (1) with compact outer layers of flat particles (2), has limited structural use. Its resistance to bending stresses is low. Screws and nails cannot be introduced into the face and only with caution into the surface.

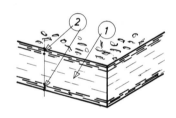

1.2.2 Laminated staircase sections

Blockboard is an excellent basis for treads (1); the front edge strip is 6–20 mm thick (2), the upper and lower veneer is at least one mm thick beneath and at least 5 mm thick above (3).

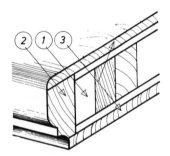

1.2.3 Glass as a material

1.2.3.1 Tempered glass
Tempered glass can be used for infill panels or risers. This type of glass is normally used in thicknesses of 8–12 mm and is cut and patterned to order.

1.2.3.2 Acrylic glass
This has the same application as tempered glass. Since it can be sawn and formed at temperatures of around 130°C., it is ideal for balustrade infills. It does, however, have the disadvantage of being a conductor of static electricity.

1.2.4 PVC tread coverings and edge strips

1.2.4.1 PVC coverings with PVC edge strips

Stairs are nearly always subject to heavy traffic and this must be taken into account when choosing coverings for them. The standard thickness for floor coverings is 2–3 mm.

In order to achieve minimum buckling in treads (*1*), a recess is cut in the edge of the tread (*4*) to take the tongue (*2*) of the PVC edge strip (*3*); the strip is then rounded against the front corner of the tread (*5*). Only the horizontal surface (*6*) should be glued in adhering the edge strip. The joint between the edge strip and the recess (*7*) should be filled with putty and the PVC covering glued down (*8*). In stairs that will be in heavy service, the joint between the covering and the edge strip is usually welded (*9*).

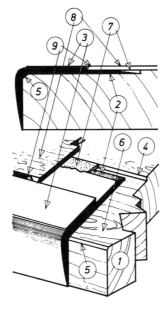

A covering and edge strip in the same plastic material creates the impression of a compact plastic unit. This method is only recommended where the tread is unlikely to warp.

1.2.4.2 PVC coverings with a wooden edge strip

A hardwood edge strip is bonded to the front edge of this PVC-covered tread. This preserves the appearance of a wooden staircase.

In this example, the covering is carried over the top edge of the hardwood strip, which affords it protection. This solution is preferable to the one above.

This three-layered covering gives the effect of a homogeneous slab. The layers should be glued one on top of the other with the appropriate amount of overlap (*1*). This method, while time-consuming, is most attractive.

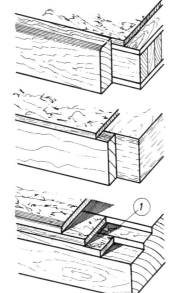

PVC coverings that are glued flush sometimes give the same impression as wallpapering, but can be used freely in lightweight stairs (*1*). Supported stairs can be covered after installation, once the treads have been screwed down from above. If the treads are solid timber, some movement should be allowed for (*2*).

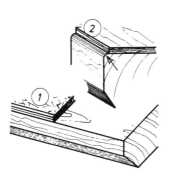

1.2.4.3 Carpet coverings

Layers of carpet need special edge strips. The front edge has to be clamped under a lip (*1*) to prevent fraying and damage. Plastic edge strips, as shown here, are resilient to wear and tear, but are not very aesthetic.

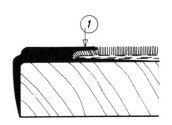

Layers of carpet on treads without PVC edge strips are particularly attractive. The edge of the step (*1*) receives the most wear, which means that only rather expensive woven carpets are suitable (tufted carpets should not be used).

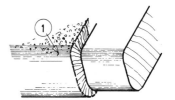

1.2.5 PVC handrails

A PVC handrail covering (*1*) is suitable for all types of balustrade. A colorful handrail can sometimes be used to good effect. Plywood makes the best core (*2*) for this type of handrail. Usual core sizes are 30 × 8 mm, 35 × 8 mm, 40 × 8 mm, and 50 × 8 mm. Handrails can be manufactured in lengths of 25 or 50 m and in a number of colors.

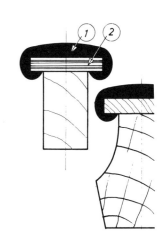

1.2.6 Metal edge strips

These strips are usually made from a light metal or brass alloy. They protect the edges of the treads and also enhance the look of the staircase.

1.2.7 PVC collars

Plastic collars or cover plates are used to cover up the junctions between circular wood or metal balusters (*1*). Button collars (*2*) can be installed after the balusters are fixed; the clip (*3*) keeps the collar firmly in place.

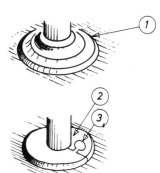

2 General Techniques of Staircase Construction

2.1 Various types of stairs and stair sections

The sketches on the facing page illustrate the most common types of ground plan for staircase construction. The basic measurements quoted here are applicable when working with a normal storey height of approximately 2.70 m.

Also illustrated is the ground plan and cross section of a stair with landing. The headroom allowed (measured vertically) should be no less than 2 m; 150 cm on very short flights (three to four steps) is recommended. The minimum clearance is measured at right angles to the pitch line. The opening between outer strings should never be less than 15 cm; otherwise it is practically impossible to mount a wreath portion at the turn of the balustrade.

Full details are given of a straight-flight, right-turn stair with a parapet meeting the stair at right angles and a wall handrail mounted on brackets. In this drawing, the various sections of a standard stair are named. The total run of a flight is calculated from the front edge of the first riser to the front edge of the last riser. Storey height (or total rise) is measured between finished floor levels.

2.2 Regulations applying to staircase construction

Readers should refer to the national and regional standard regulations, local authority ordinances, and those of individual towns concerning staircase and building constructions.

Both the American National Standards Institute and the British Standards Institution produce detailed publications setting out specific codes of practice pertaining to types of stairs, required heights in high-rise buildings, domestic stairs, lighting, safety regulations, tables of moisture content of wood, the structural use of timber, steel, or aluminum, and so on.

In multi-family dwellings, runs of no more than eighteen steps should occur between landings or half-landings; in single-family dwellings, no more than sixteen steps are recommended. Stairs should have a clear headroom (measured vertically) of 2.10 m.

Where steps are tapered, a tread width of at least 100 mm should occur at a distance of no less than 150 mm from the narrowest part of the tread. Where the going width is less than 260 mm, an overlap of at least 30 mm should occur between steps. In the case of goings of 260 mm and more, an overlap is advisable.

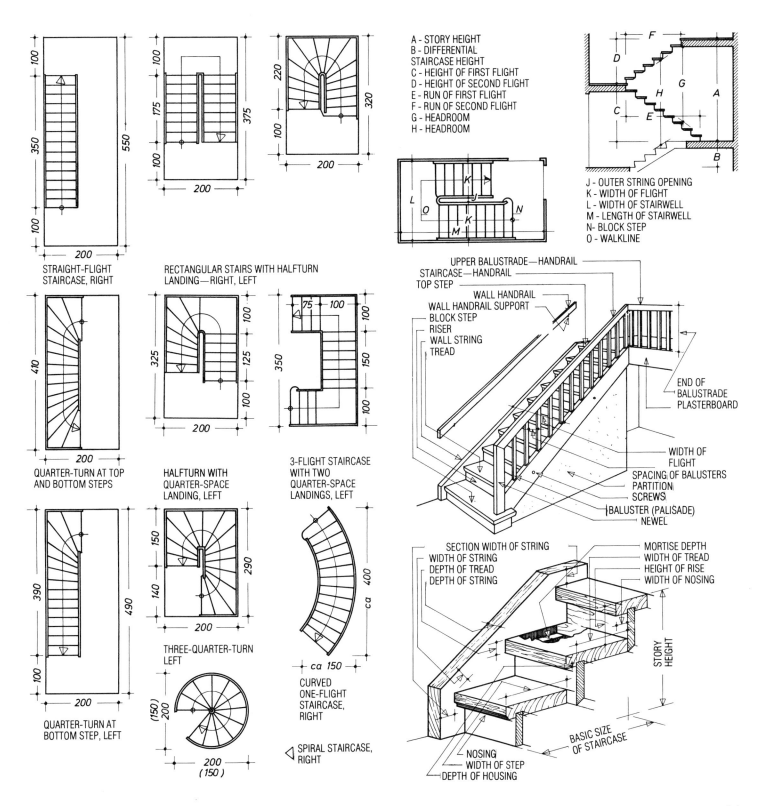

STRAIGHT-FLIGHT
STAIRCASE, RIGHT

RECTANGULAR STAIRS WITH HALFTURN
LANDING—RIGHT, LEFT

QUARTER-TURN AT TOP
AND BOTTOM STEPS

HALFTURN WITH
QUARTER-SPACE
LANDING, LEFT

3-FLIGHT STAIRCASE
WITH TWO
QUARTER-SPACE
LANDINGS, LEFT

QUARTER-TURN AT
BOTTOM STEP, LEFT

THREE-QUARTER-TURN
LEFT

CURVED
ONE-FLIGHT
STAIRCASE,
RIGHT

◁ SPIRAL STAIRCASE,
RIGHT

A - STORY HEIGHT
B - DIFFERENTIAL
STAIRCASE HEIGHT
C - HEIGHT OF FIRST FLIGHT
D - HEIGHT OF SECOND FLIGHT
E - RUN OF FIRST FLIGHT
F - RUN OF SECOND FLIGHT
G - HEADROOM
H - HEADROOM

J - OUTER STRING OPENING
K - WIDTH OF FLIGHT
L - WIDTH OF STAIRWELL
M - LENGTH OF STAIRWELL
N - BLOCK STEP
O - WALKLINE

UPPER BALUSTRADE—HANDRAIL
STAIRCASE—HANDRAIL
TOP STEP
WALL HANDRAIL
WALL HANDRAIL SUPPORT
BLOCK STEP
RISER
WALL STRING
TREAD

END OF
BALUSTRADE
PLASTERBOARD

WIDTH OF
FLIGHT
SPACING OF BALUSTERS
PARTITION
SCREWS
BALUSTER (PALISADE)
NEWEL

SECTION WIDTH OF STRING
WIDTH OF STRING
DEPTH OF TREAD
DEPTH OF STRING

MORTISE DEPTH
WIDTH OF TREAD
HEIGHT OF RISE
WIDTH OF NOSING

STORY
HEIGHT

BASIC SIZE
OF STAIRCASE

NOSING
WIDTH OF STEP
DEPTH OF HOUSING

11

2.3 Ground rules of staircase construction

2.3.1 Rise ratio

The ratio is as follows: 2 rises (R) + 1 going (G) should equal between 60 and 64 cm (the standard is 63 cm). Ideal dimensions for a domestic staircase are: R = 18 cm, G = 27 cm (i.e., 2 × 18 = 36 + 27 = 63 cm).

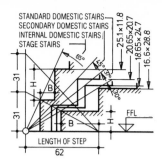

2.3.2 Pitch

The pitch of a stair where the rise equals 18 cm and the going equals 27 cm is approximately 34% and, interestingly, this gives a ratio of two times the story height (3.00 m) or rise (18 cm) to three times the run (4.50 m) or going (27 cm). This formula (2:3) can be used for deciding measurements by graphic or mathematical methods.

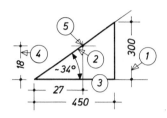

2.3.3 Walkline

The walkline of a stair is the line followed by a person in using the stair (1). Its length provides the basic measure from which the length of the going is calculated and can therefore be applied to the ground plan when the stair is curved (2). A measurement taken from the center of the handrail to the walkline (3) is normally 45 cm and in narrower stairs it often coincides with the center line of the stair. In order to avoid confusion, the nosing of the tread is only indicated over the strings (4).

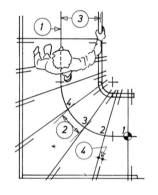

2.3.4 Widths

The width is determined by the number of people likely to use the stair at any one time.

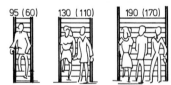

2.3.5 Length of stair (run)

A run is a sequence of more than three steps before a landing occurs; a landing must be built after eighteen rises.

2.3.6 Landings

The length of a landing should not be less than the unobstructed width of the stairs. In steeper stairs, where smaller steps are taken, landings can be correspondingly narrower. Landings should be wide enough to allow stretchers or furniture to be carried.

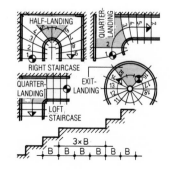

2.3.7 Dimension of treads

Treads over 26 cm deep do not need a nosing. In tapered stairs, a width of at least 10 cm at a distance of 15 cm from the narrowest point of the tread is obligatory.

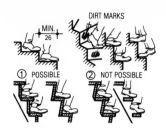

2.3.8 Headroom

Determination of the headroom in curved or spiral stairs is often difficult and should be shown in a schematic sketch. In plans, a stair-thickness of 25 cm should be taken, from which the headroom is calculated parallel with the strings at a vertical height of 2.10 m. In this way the points of intersection with the ceiling are found and the ceiling recesses determined.

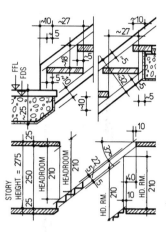

2.3.9 Designation of left and right

The designation of a stair as left or right results from the direction in which the run turns from the lowest level. Stairs that lead upwards in a clockwise direction are right stairs. Stairs that run in a counterclockwise direction are known as left stairs.

2.4 Safety standards for stairs and balustrades

2.4.1 Fire precautions

The terms flammable, inflammable, nonflammable, and so on, denote the degree of resistance to fire of the various components. In addition, certain of them are termed fire-resistant or fire-proof. In this latter category belong stairs made of sandstone, brick, concrete, and reinforced concrete up to 10 cm thick; oak (hardwood); steel with fire-proof covering; as well as timber and stone stairs, if they are fire-proofed on the underside, for example, with plaster applied to a depth of 3 cm on cladding, piping, or metal surfaces. Metals with a low melting point should not be used for escape stairs. Stone staircases when subjected to heat give no warning of collapse and, unless specially treated, should not be used.

2.4.2 Insulation against noise

Carpet and PVC coverings greatly reduce noise in stairs. Where the underside of the stair is plastered, a filling of rock wool is used between the plaster, the underside of the tread, and the back edge of the riser as a noise conductor. Underlays of rubber, felt, or foam plastic all have a noise-reducing effect.

2.4.3 Stability

Loading of stairs in domestic use—350 Kg/m²
Loading of stairs in commercial use—500 Kg/m²
Details to be noted: Junctions of string elements, such as newels and landing connections, should have four to eight dowels sunk at

points of connection. Recommended minimum tread thicknesses in free mortised treads are as follows:

Tread length up to 80 cm—4.5 cm thickness.
Tread length up to 90 cm—5.0 cm thickness.
Tread length up to 100 cm—5.7 cm thickness.
Tread length up to 110 cm—6.5 cm thickness.

The balustrade should be able to withstand lateral stress of 50 Kg/m².

2.4.4 The use of adequate lighting to ensure safety

Since dark stairs in dimly lit stairwells greatly increase the danger of falling, treads should either be light in color or light edge strips should be used to indicate where the front edges of treads fall. Lighting should not be too sharp. Stairs of less than three rises, or single steps, can be easily overlooked and present a hazard. Open-riser stairs allow light to pass through and give an overall lighter effect. A minimum illumination of 150x for general stairs and 100lx for domestic stairs is recommended.

2.4.5 Non-slip surfaces

As oiled or waxed surfaces are far too slippery and present too great an accident risk, they contravene building regulations. PVC coverings should be cleaned only with those cleaning agents recommended by the manufacturers. Sealed surfaces can be cleaned with luke-warm water. Harsh or oily cleaning agents should not be applied since once they have been used the surface can never be resealed.

2.4.6 Safety regulations relating to balustrades

Standard balustrade height is 90 cm or 84 cm in single dwellings, measured from the front edge of the tread to the top edge of the handrail. The clear distance between balusters or other infills should be 12 cm at the most. At its thinnest point, a wooden baluster should have a diameter of at least 20 mm. Horizontal boards should be avoided since they tempt children to climb them. The thickness of the handrail should be such that it can withstand lateral stress of 50 Kg/m². Handrails should be made of hardwood. In stairs of less than five rises, a handrail is not obligatory, but it is nevertheless recommended. Where stairs are more than 1.25 m wide, a handrail should be mounted on both sides. Height differentials (e.g., ramps) of more than 1.00 m require a parapet. Wall handrails should be mounted at least 4 cm from the wall.

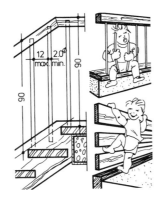

2.4.7 Creaking stairs

Creaking in stairs is caused by wooden surfaces rubbing together. It is possible to avoid this by using warp-free woods and gluing the junctions of tread and riser. Where treads are only lightly supported they will bend slightly in use and produce a creaking effect in rubbing against the mortises in the string. To prevent this, mortise grooves, notches in strings, and other junction points can usefully be lined with felt, rubber, or foam plastic.

2.4.8 Clear distances between treads

Clear distances should not exceed 10 cm. In staircases that will be used by small children, it is particularly important to keep as far within this limit as possible. In stairs located in schools or other public buildings, this measurement should be reduced to 6 cm, so that bottles cannot roll through.

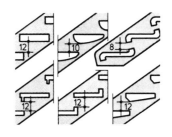

3 Types of Staircase Construction

3.1 Closed-string stairs

3.1.1 Mortised stairs

Risers and treads are mortised to a depth of around 2 cm into the 5–6-cm deep string. The stair is affixed by means of approximately 10-mm screws throughout.

3.1.2 Mortised open-riser stairs

In this variation without risers, the visible screws can be sunk into the treads.

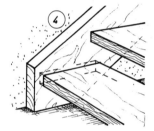

3.1.3 Stairs set into strings

The strings are notched to take the treads—an old form of construction which is being revived.

3.1.4 Design variations on the above

(*1*) The treads have been dovetailed and wedged.
(*2*) In addition, treads notched.
(*3*) Treads notched, corner cut away and screwed into position.

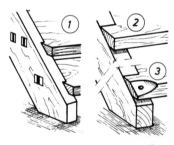

3.1.5 Inserted stairs

This construction is used when the depth of the string is insufficient to allow treads to be set into it.

3:1.6 Stair screwed in position

The treads and risers in this stair, which are about 6–8 cm thick, are carpeted above and below and bolted into steel strings.

3.2 Cut-string stairs

3.2.1 Cut-string stairs with open risers

The strings are notched from the top and are only statically effective at the lower sections. Care must be taken in the case of long strings.

3.2.2 Cut-string stairs with risers

Overhang on outer string side
(a) Risers—approximately 3 cm
(b) Treads—approximately 5–6 cm

3.2.3 Cut-string stairs—risers mitred to strings (*1*)

This type of stair is only to be recommended where treads and risers are laminated.

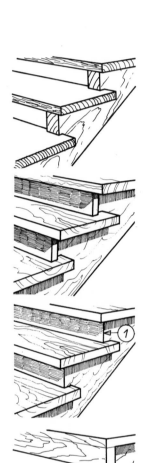

3.2.4 Cut-string stairs with overhanging treads and risers

Laminated treads and risers are firmly plugged together and glued, then glued and plugged to the recessed beams (strings).

3.2.5 Cut-string stairs with sectioned-string facades

This allows solid wood treads to shrink away from the back without a warp joint being directly visible.

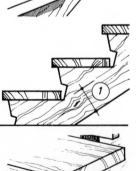

3.2.6 Cut-string stairs with safety bands

In this variation, intermediate bands act as a safety barrier and can be affixed to the upper or lower edge of the tread.

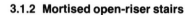

3.3 String stairs with inclined soffits and brackets

3.3.1 String stairs with plugged wooden brackets

The tread is screwed on from the underside of the bracket, then the tread and bracket are plugged to the soffit.

3.3.2 String stairs with pincer-type soffits

This is a modern construction with a rustic appearance; it lends itself to temporary stairs since it can also be nailed together.

3.3.3 String stairs with tread supports

Round wooden dowels (approximately 30–35 mm) support the treads at four points; in this construction, laminated treads must be used.

3.3.4 Stairs supported on steel bearer angles

This provides a solid and stable connection between string and treads.

3.3.5 String stairs supported by balusters

The strings are recessed and the undersides of the treads are plugged. Then both balusters and the ends of the treads are notched, plugged, and glued.

3.3.6 Block steps

Both treads and strings are laminated and connected by heavy-duty plugs. This method is especially suitable for large staircase constructions.

3.3.7 Treads notched to take baluster boards

Tube sockets have been sunk into the facings of the treads, since wooden plugs would not hold firm in facing or cross-grained wood. Instead of screws, whose heads are left visible here, wooden dowels (approximately 20 mm) could be sunk into the sockets, their heads protruding about 5–10 mm beyond the surface of the boards.

3.4 Stairs with suspended treads

In the examples that follow, the handrail acts as the load-bearing element of the staircase. Using this method, if skillfully executed, a low-price lightweight stair can be constructed. It is most advantageous if the handrail can be given a supplementary anchoring at its point of intersection with the ceiling (1). This considerably diminishes the length of loading (2). The balusters act as a safety barrier.

3.4.1 Stairs with suspended treads, using tubular steel tension rods

The newel post supports the lower part of the handrail. The tension rods attached to the handrail each connect two treads with each other. These tension rods can be approximately 20–22-mm-thick steel rods; they run through the treads and are horizontally bolted or screwed to them. In stairs that will be subject to constant loading, they can be manufactured from rolled steel with threaded bolts (several examples are contained in the picture section of this book). The board between the rods is merely a safety precaution.

3.4.2 Stairs with suspended treads with hardwood tension rods

The tension rods shown here are somewhat daring. A heavy-duty plug holds the construction at the point of contact. It is most important that there be sufficient timber thickness between the plug and the end of the rod in order not to split the timber when loading is imposed on the staircase. The handrail cross section is T- or L-shaped, so that the pressure zone at the top of the handrail is reinforced against lateral buckling.

3.4.3 Staircases with suspended treads with sheet steel tension rods and cross pieces

The last illustration shows a solid welded construction consisting of approximately 10 × 40 mm flat rods, which are affixed laterally to the handrail.

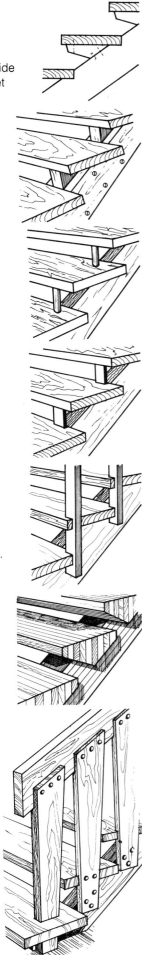

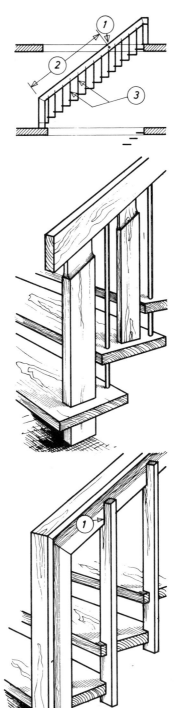

3.5 Spine-string stairs

If two flights are positioned one above the other, the string follows the walkline, i.e., it hangs directly above the head of anyone using the lower flight; in such cases it is preferable to construct a stair with two strings.

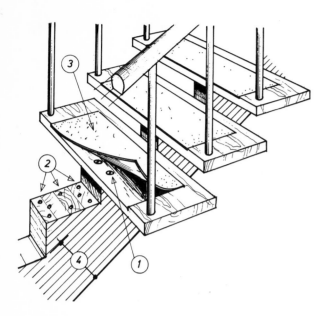

3.5.1 Spine-string stair with laminated timber string

The treads are fixed with heavy-duty (about 8/80 mm) woodscrews (*1*). Six or eight screws are necessary for each tread (*2*). When the covering is later glued in position, the screws are concealed (*3*).

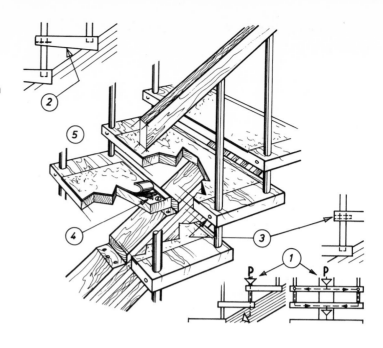

3.5.3 Spine-string stair with balustrade support rods

The stress of loading on the treads is transmitted through the banister rods to the back edge of the treads beneath (*1*), and from there into the string. A conical tread cross section (*2*) is not only functional but also most attractive. The banister rods run through the treads and are screwed or plugged to these (*3*). The treads should be screwed to the string in several places (*4*). The covering (PVC or carpet), which can be laid down after installation of the stair, conceals the heads of the screws (*5*).

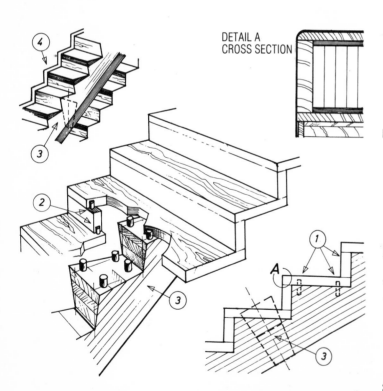

DETAIL A
CROSS SECTION

3.5.2 Spine-string stair with folded "concertina" treads

This construction is neat and clean-edged. Treads and risers must be laminated (*Detail A*), so that they can be plugged (*1* and *2*) to the spine string (*3*), which has been precut in conical shapes. The stair gives the impression of a piece of origami or fluting (*4*).

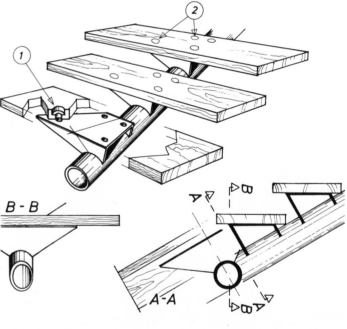

3.5.4 Stair with tubular steel string

The diameter of the tube must be of adequate dimensions, not only to prevent bending but also to act against torsion. Here, the treads (*1*) are fixed by bolting to 10-mm-thick sheet steel brackets welded to the steel tube. The bore holes in the surface of the brackets should be big enough to allow a solid tread to shear slightly following installation.

1.3 Types of wood—color and properties

Pine

Rough-grained with hard (brownish) and soft (whitish) growth rings, pine lends itself particularly well to construction purposes.

Red Pine

A light, soft wood from the southeastern portion of the United States, red pine is not particularly durable and therefore limited in uses in construction. It has a straight grain.

Scotch Fir

This wood is structurally similar to the indigenous pine but heavier and with a relatively high resin content. There is a considerable difference in color between the heartwood and the sapwood and thus it is unsuitable for curved strings.

Gaboon (Okoumé)

This wood from West Africa (Gabon) is frequently used in the manufacture of blockboard or plywood. Ideal for laminated strings or wreath pieces; it is long-grained and warps very little. Its use in construction is limited.

Larch

This is a hard wood with a high resin content. Care must be taken with the light sap zones.

Afara (Limba)

Widely used as a veneer for doors, afara is from Central America. A soft wood, it is virtually knot-free. It stains very well and is extremely durable, but has limited use.

Ash

In this tough, flexible wood, a great difference exists between heartwood and sapwood. It has a rough-pored structure. The sapwood tends to react to light penetration by discoloring and becoming yellowish and should therefore be protected against this.

Afzelia (Doussié)

This West African wood is ideal for building staircases. The heartwood is usually creviced; the sapwood is light in color but darkens in the sun. It warps very little and is extremely durable. Afzelia is comparable with oak.

Maple

Its thick texture makes maple ideal for surface treatments (also for staining). It has a strong tendency to turn yellow and must therefore be treated with a light-filtering substance. It is very suitable for balusters.

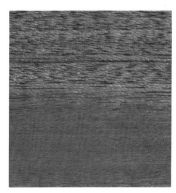

Mahogany

Sapeli mahogany is striped, while Sipi mahogany is mottled. This wood from West Africa is excellent for use in staircases, and is extremely durable.

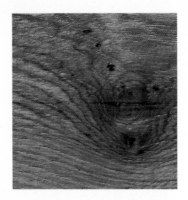

Teak

Its high content of thin liquid resin makes this wood from Burma, Thailand, and Java particularly resistant to decomposition and insect attack. The silica contained in the wood makes working difficult. The surface should be treated only with special oil. It is an ideal wood for staircases.

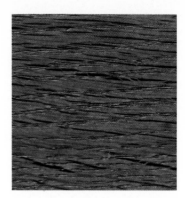

Darkened (Fumed) Oak

A penetration of 2–3 mm is recommended (i.e., approximately three days exposure to ammonia fumes in hermetically sealed chambers) for treads, strings, and other sections.

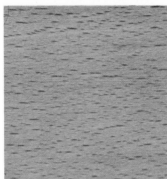

Steamed Beech

The reddish color is obtained by exposure to acid fumes after cutting, this process also gives the beech greater durability and evens out the difference between the dark heartwood and light sapwood.

Lime-washed Oak

This wood is only suitable for larger surfaces (strings, risers, or infill panels). A pore filler is applied across the grain with a rough cloth after priming; finally, the surface is treated with a thin layer of varnish.

Oak

An ideal wood for all parts of the staircase, oak is rough-pored and short-grained; it is extremely durable and resistant to weathering and decay. The white sapwood should not be used.

Stained and Lime-washed Oak

The best surface effects are achieved through a combination of stain and pore filler since this maximizes the color contrast between the dark surfaces and the lighter pores.

1.4 Wood in the living area

This suspended stair has been manufactured in four sections with eight rises each and is hung by suspension rods at the points where the segments join; it is also supported at floor level and at the landing trimmer. These latter two points can sustain stress in all three directions, but the middle supports (suspension rods) are only able to sustain stress in the vertical axis. Momentum cannot be transmitted to the individual support points. The strings are screwed to the treads to prevent shearing. The individual staircase segments act in the horizontal plane, thus rendering the construction suitably stable.

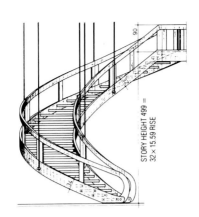

STORY HEIGHT 499 =
32 × 15.59 RISE

90

34

Color and form complement each other in this staircase. The mat-white steel rods with their brass cuffs are especially appealing and a cozy atmosphere is created by carpeting the wooden steps—a good combination with the textured wallpaper used in the stairwell.

3.6 Spiral staircases

3.6.1 Spiral staircases without a central column

Although this stair has no central newel or column, it falls into the category of spiral staircases since, on the ground plan, its treads all emanate from one point. In this example, treads and risers must be laminated (1).

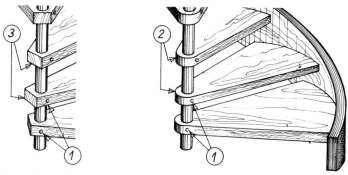

3.6.2 Spiral staircases with central tubular steel columns

Treads are bolted to the tube (1) with approximately 6–10-mm bolts. Where heavier loading is anticipated, spacer sleeves should be installed.

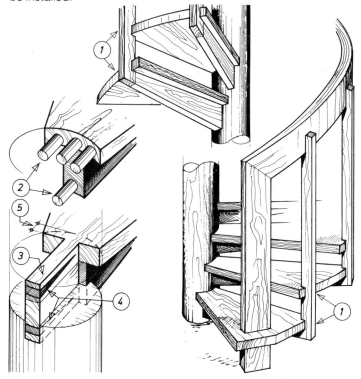

3.6.3 Spiral stairs with cantilevered brackets

Treads and brackets are plugged (2) or dovetailed by hand (3), glued, and wedged (4).

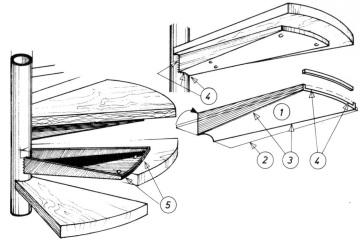

3.6.4 Spiral staircase with tubular steel column and sheet steel brackets

The brackets (1) are cut out (3) of rectangular sheets (2) and welded to the column (4). The treads are screwed in position from beneath the brackets (5).

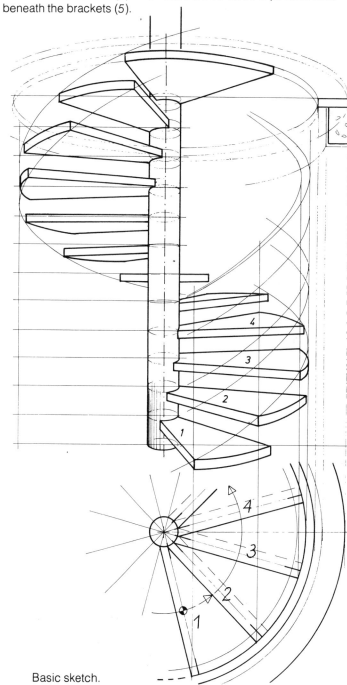

Basic sketch.

3.6.5 Types of spiral staircases

The ground plans below are drawn to the scale of 1:50 and can be transferred directly to working drawings. In the 150 types there are three treads to each quarter-circular walkline; in types 175 to 200, there are three and one-half. The ideal going: rise ratio, resulting from the relation of tread width to rise in these examples, forms the basis for the heights recommended in this table.

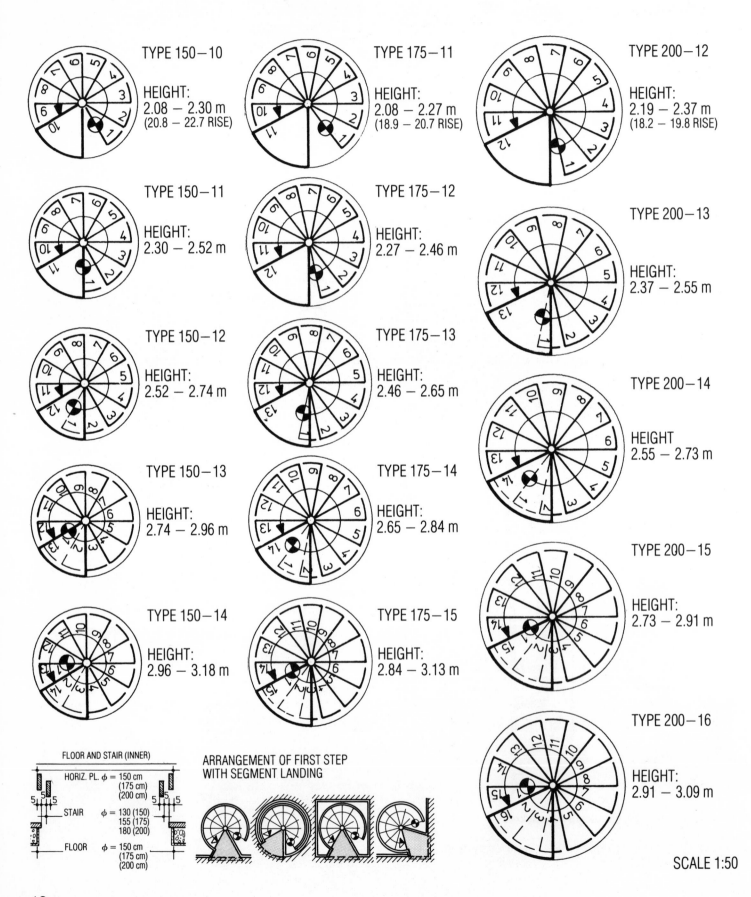

TYPE 150—10

HEIGHT:
2.08 — 2.30 m
(20.8 — 22.7 RISE)

TYPE 150—11

HEIGHT:
2.30 — 2.52 m

TYPE 150—12

HEIGHT:
2.52 — 2.74 m

TYPE 150—13

HEIGHT:
2.74 — 2.96 m

TYPE 150—14

HEIGHT:
2.96 — 3.18 m

TYPE 175—11

HEIGHT:
2.08 — 2.27 m
(18.9 — 20.7 RISE)

TYPE 175—12

HEIGHT:
2.27 — 2.46 m

TYPE 175—13

HEIGHT:
2.46 — 2.65 m

TYPE 175—14

HEIGHT:
2.65 — 2.84 m

TYPE 175—15

HEIGHT:
2.84 — 3.13 m

TYPE 200—12

HEIGHT:
2.19 — 2.37 m
(18.2 — 19.8 RISE)

TYPE 200—13

HEIGHT:
2.37 — 2.55 m

TYPE 200—14

HEIGHT
2.55 — 2.73 m

TYPE 200—15

HEIGHT:
2.73 — 2.91 m

TYPE 200—16

HEIGHT:
2.91 — 3.09 m

FLOOR AND STAIR (INNER)

HORIZ. PL. φ = 150 cm
(175 cm)
(200 cm)

5 5 5   5 5 5

STAIR   φ = 130 (150)
155 (175)
180 (200)

FLOOR   φ = 150 cm
(175 cm)
(200 cm)

ARRANGEMENT OF FIRST STEP
WITH SEGMENT LANDING

SCALE 1:50

18

3.7 Space-saving stairs

Steep-set stairs, built along conventional lines, create problems in use, particularly in descent. The leg touches the middle tread (1) as it descends and makes contact with the bottom step (2). The ball of the foot is left hanging (3). The danger of falling is very great, but there is a solution to the problem: if the tread that is missed each time by one foot is kept narrow (4), its front edge is no longer a hindrance and the danger of falling greatly decreases. This means, however, that the stair must always be negotiated with the same foot first.

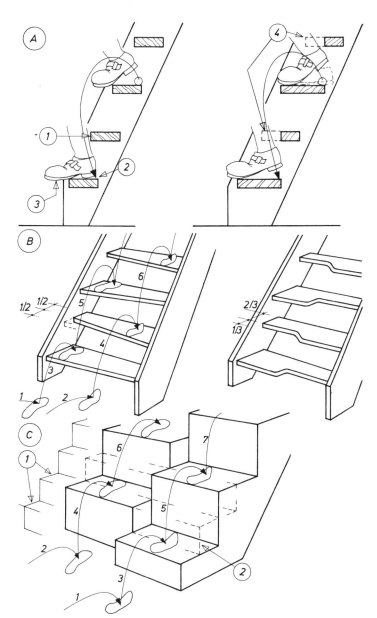

3.8 Various stair constructions

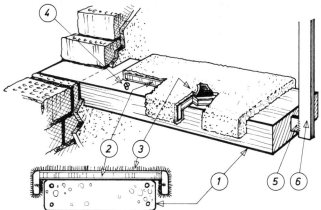

3.8.1 Stairs with cantilevered treads

Concrete slabs (1) are fixed in a 24-cm-thick wall. U- or bathtub-shaped laminated timbers (blockboard) (2), carpeted (3) make an unusual covering for the treads. Bedded mountings (4) hold the board in place on the cantilevered concrete slab.

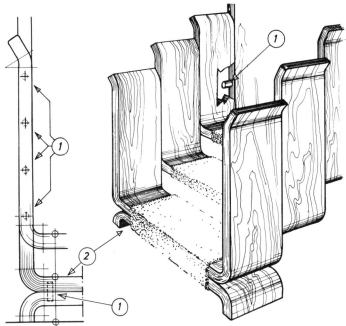

3.8.2 Stairs with molded veneer sections

These sections are made from veneers bent around formers and bonded together. Plugs must be used in the connection of the vertical sections.

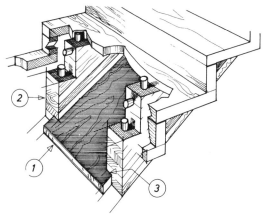

3.8.3 Box beam string stair

The load-bearing element here consists of two bearing beams (2) and a layer of blockboard (1).

19

4 Types of Balustrade Construction

Safety is the main function of balustrades. Distances between balusters or guardrails and the height of the balustrade are determined by the prevailing regulations for construction.

4.1 Types of balustrade

4.1.1 Balustrades with laterally fixed wooden or metal balusters

4.1.1.1 Balustrades with laterally fixed wooden balusters—no infill panels

Simple, regular constructions with many variations are a possibility. The retaining rods can be invisibly plugged or visibly screwed in position.

4.1.1.2 Balustrade with laterally fixed steel retaining rods and guardrail

The cross section of the steel baluster, sideways onto the stair, is approximately 10 × 40 mm. Its cross section lengthwise to the stair is approximately 15 × 40 mm square to the stair; its dimensions are 22 × 22 mm. The guardrail should be at least 22 mm thick. Strings, handrail, and guardrail are all screwed in position from the stair side. Balustrades with these types of retaining rods do not need a newel post. The handrail and guardrail can be constructed and fixed either as a framework or as individual elements.

4.1.1.3 Balustrade with laterally fixed steel balusters

This type of stair has a rolled steel gate as an infill. The balustrade gives a lightweight effect and should therefore be employed where the stairwell is narrow. The stability along the length of the stair is less than it would be if a guardrail was present, so the newel post must bear the loading in this direction.

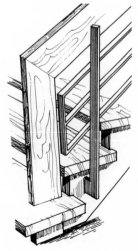

4.1.2 Balustrades with rods

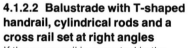

4.1.2.1 Balustrade with an L-shaped handrail and cylindrical wooden or metal rods

Thin rods should be drilled in to a depth of 6–7 cm; they then act as tensioned supports.

4.1.2.2 Balustrade with T-shaped handrail, cylindrical rods and a cross rail set at right angles

If the cross rail is mounted in the lower section of the thin rods, it gives them greater stability.

4.1.2.3 Balustrade with oval handrail and tapered rods

This traditional type of balustrade can be most attractive provided that the newel post and handrail blend in style. In differentiating between rods and balusters, the following definitions apply: a rod is round, turned, and up to 40 mm in diameter; a baluster is more than 40 mm in diameter and can have a round, square, or rectangular cross section.

4.1.3 Infill panels

4.1.3.1 Baluster—string elements with infill panels of tempered or acrylic glass

As the sketch shows, this is an example of stair and balustrade working as a single unit. In order to avoid unattractive glass edges being visible, the panels should be built in prior to the assembly and gluing of the sections. Although the rounding of edges here has required a great deal of effort, it gives the stair a most attractive finish.

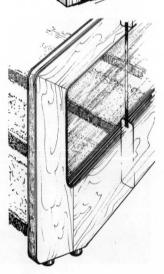

4.2 Handrail profiles

Nowadays, handrails are usually shaped from a rectangular piece of wood. The handrail should be easy to grip (the most comfortable grip is circular, between 45–50-mm diameter) so that old people, particularly, can feel confident in using the stairs. Its form should blend with the style of the stair, and its thickness will depend on its length, considering the load it must withstand (50 Kg/m² of horizontal pressure). The profile chosen will depend partly on whether the handrail is straight or curved. Handrails are generally made from hardwood and their surfaces should be mat-finished, so that they do not become "greasy" quickly.

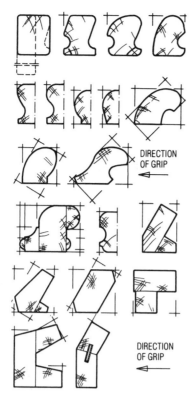

DIRECTION OF GRIP

DIRECTION OF GRIP

4.3 Wall handrail profiles

The distance from the wall must be at least 4 cm. Depth of grip should be approximately 8 cm. A lighting strip behind the handrail is interesting from an architectonic viewpoint and has safety value in addition. Care should be taken where walls are badly plastered; in order to overcome this defect, a cloudy effect can be created by illuminating the surface.

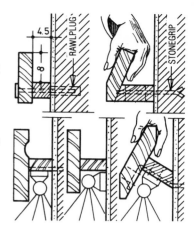

4.4 Decorative handrails

Despite new fashions, classic stairs are still much in demand. The "snail" is designed in the following way: 12-mm squares are drawn from a central point on the lower edge of the handrail. At its thickest point, the snail equals one segment (1) at a radius level with the handrail. Following quarter-circles are each 12 mm less in radius and lead eventually to the middle of the snail.

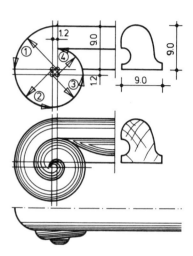

4.5 Rods and balusters

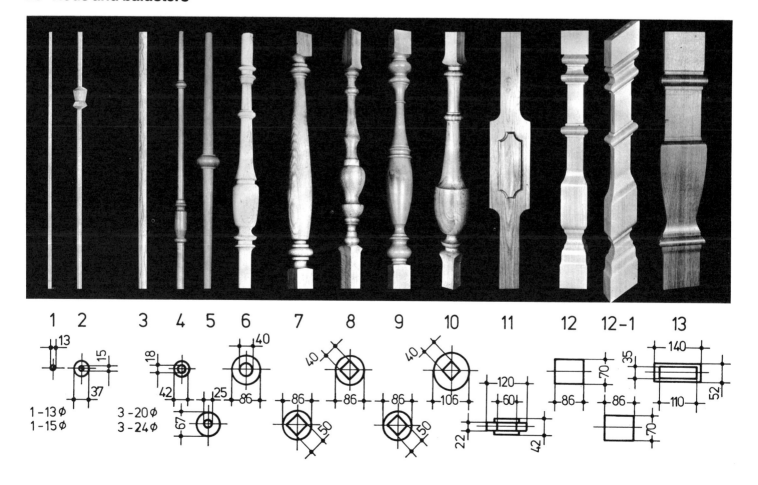

21

5 Staircase Details

5.1 Stairs with landing

5.1.1

The offsetting of treads in the top and bottom steps creates an ideal connection between landing and flight in slab stairs with landing (1).

5.1.2

By employing the same method, cut-string stairs with timber-bearing beams can be connected to ceilings or landings using steel bearer angles.

5.1.3

Laminated strings are neatly jointed at their points of intersection (1), which makes possible the clean lines demanded by modern staircase design.

5.1.4

Alignment of the lines of nosings at top and bottom steps (1) is advisable in the case of mortised or partially mortised string stairs. The combined width of top and bottom steps runs across the entire width of the stairwell.

5.1.5

In straight landing posts at the turn of the stair, the level of points of intersection of the nosing line should correspond with the inner level of the posts (1). This means that the points of intersection of strings and handrails fall along the same line. With this fact in mind, the stair should first be drawn in detail; the recessing of the ceilings and landings can then be determined.

5.1.6

The most space-saving stair with landing is achieved by setting the landing post as near to the flight as the edges of top and bottom steps will allow (1). In the example shown, approximately 13 cm are gained on each landing and ceiling width. However, this makes an undesirable offsetting of vertical thrust in the height unavoidable (2).

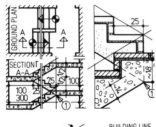

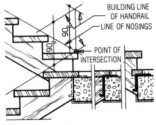

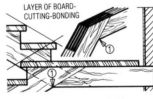

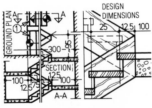

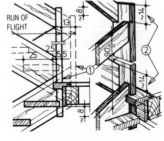

5.2 Wooden landings with wreath portions

5.2.1 Semicircular wreaths

An attractive string ramp can only be produced if the landing width (P.BR.) corresponds with the normal tread width (approximately 25 cm) at the center point of the string wreath (*Sketch A*). In order to achieve an attractive curve where the stairs are plastered on the underside, the lower corner must be bevelled (1). Runs with a landing should also be reinforced against collapse by the use of heavy-duty steel bearer angles (2). In Sketch B, the landing width has been drawn too wide on the ground plan and this produces a distorted string ramp. The development of the string in Sketch C is even worse. Here, the landing width is much too narrow. In order to conceal the turning point, the corner of the outer string can be carried down (5) or up (6). This improves the line of the ramp, but is more time-consuming from a technical point of view. The string developments illustrated on the right very clearly show the types of mistakes often made in practice.

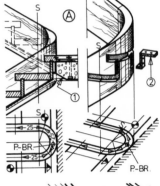

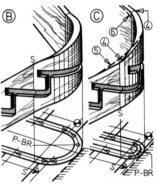

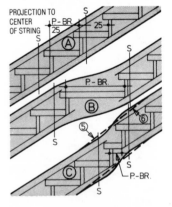

5.2.2 Quarter-circular wreaths

As with semicircular wreaths, an attractive string ramp (7) results when the tread and landing widths correspond, measured at the central point of the string (8). If the landing width is too narrow (9), an unattractive effect is produced in the ramp (10).

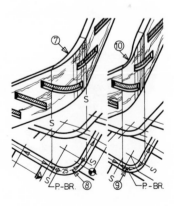

5.3 Top and bottom steps—details

5.3.1 Bottom steps—newel posts

The wall string is notched to house the notch in the side of the newel. The blockstep is pushed into position from the front. Vertical thrust acting on string and newel posts achieves a high degree of lateral stability and this is increased by the fixing of string to tread (2).

5.3.2 The top step

5.3.2.1

The newel post at the top step connects the parapet to the balustrade at right angles (1). The points of intersection of the balustrade should be aligned if possible. A top newel post is not essential in the connection of a parapet (2), but a smooth transitional joint with the balustrade (3) should be made if a newel is not present.

5.3.2.2 Parapets

Parapets which run parallel to the balustrade require a connecting post (1), in order to avoid lateral instability when the raking members are installed. The height of the balustrade at the top corner should coincide with the height of the parapet (2).

5.3.3 The top step—junction with floor

Shown here are the (1) PVC edge strip, (2) nosing, (3) blockboard or chipboard, (4) PVC covering, (5) underlay, (6) infrastructure, (7) plywood, (8) parquet, (9) bearer angle every 30 cm, (10) stone layer, and (11) flooring (needs no insulation at the top step).

5.4 Fixing Details

5.4.1 Screwing treads to strings

(1) Long tension screws cause problems at angled points of connection (A). A better solution where treads are tapered is the use of short tension elements (2), e.g., short anchors (3), carriage bolts sunk into the treads (4) with hemispherical washers (5) and nuts (6). The hole is concealed by a cross-grained wooden plug (7). Since it is invisible on the surface of the tread, the screw and flat nut of the author's own design (8 and 9) are ideal for this purpose. The hole is cut with a special cutter on a long-hole drill (10); the screw is then inserted along the longitudinal cut (11).

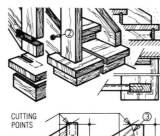
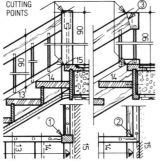
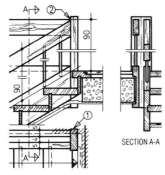
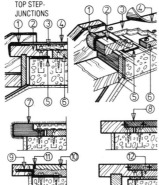
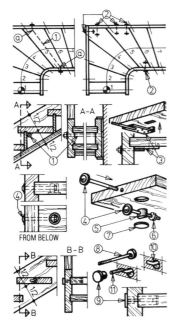

5.4.2 Hanging the strings

Fixing with a split standard keeps the top step flush with the floor (1), together with a steel bolt (2), and (3) a bearer angle (a thin layer of felt can be inserted to prevent creaking).

5.4.3 Fixing corners

The corners of wall strings are fixed by using special wall joints (1), split standards (2), by drilling in steel bolts (3), or by plugging (4).

5.4.4 Fixing treads to the wall

Treads can be fixed to the wall by: double brackets with split standards (1), in which a longitudinal slot allows for some movement following installation (2), notching (3), single split standard for laminated treads (4), treads screwed in position from below (5); an invisible screw in a laminated tread (6) groove-cut with long-hole drill (7), sleeve set in facing (8); an invisible screw in a solid-wood tread (9), using bearer angle (10), allowing for possible warping (11), angling of screw is preferable (12).

5.4.5 Fixing the handrail to the wall

Shown here are notched handrail facing (1), insertion of plugged brass angle (2), and screwing (3). Also shown is an invisible fixing by filling in the hole housing the split standard (4).

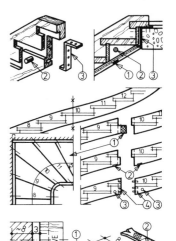
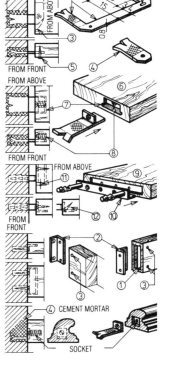

5.5 Connecting wall strings to the wall

Shown are attachments by rabbets (1), rabbets set behind the string (2), rabbets flush with string, plastered (3), and a free-standing wall string (4).

5.6 Infill panels

5.6.1 Glass infills

Shown here are (1) replaceable glass; (2) metal clamps (do not use aluminum since it will melt and the glass will fall out), on a (3) steel baseplate; and (4) a wooden clamp.

5.6.2 Wooden infills

These can be a plain infill (1), a plain infill with decorative beading affixed (2), infills notched into balusters (3), and notched into baluster boards (4). The balusters illustrated here can be inserted vertically between glass or wooden infills.

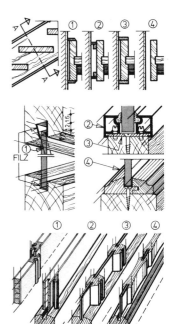

6 Staircases

6.1 Straight-flight stairs and stairs with landings

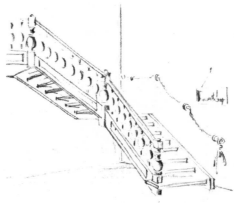

The design of a staircase should be compatible with the overall style of the house. The farmhouse stair shown top left creates a rustic effect, in contrast to the elegant, stylized stair shown to its right. At bottom left, the drawing illustrates a solid, dependable staircase which is classically timeless in its conception; the staircase and landing illustrated bottom center are given a functional appearance by a very positive use of wide boards in the strings and handrails. Note the absence of newel posts. The staircase shown bottom right is an experimental construction, made up of layers of wood glued together vertically, and this should provide inspiration for the development of further designs.

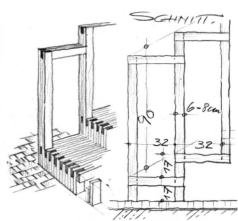

STAIRS AND BANISTER
BONDED PLYWOOD
FLOOR—PARQUET

6.1.1 Straight-flight string stairs with landings

This flight of stairs, which is carpet-covered throughout, connects a large living room on the lower floor with another on the upper floor. The simple line of the strings, which have been painted white, blends equally well with furnishings in either classic or ultra-modern styles.

FIRST STEP—DETAIL

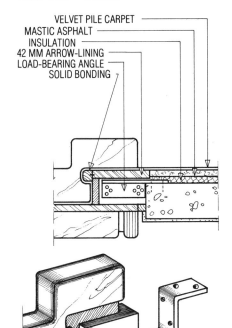

VELVET PILE CARPET
MASTIC ASPHALT
INSULATION
42 MM ARROW-LINING
LOAD-BEARING ANGLE
SOLID BONDING

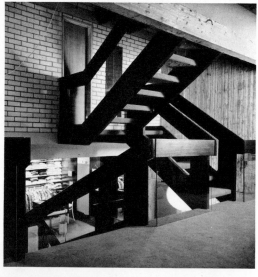

These open-riser stairs connecting five floors in a clothing store are made of mahogany. The infill panels are 12-mm-thick tempered glass. Floors and treads are carpeted. The steel bearer angles are screwed in before the strings and newel posts are glued together.

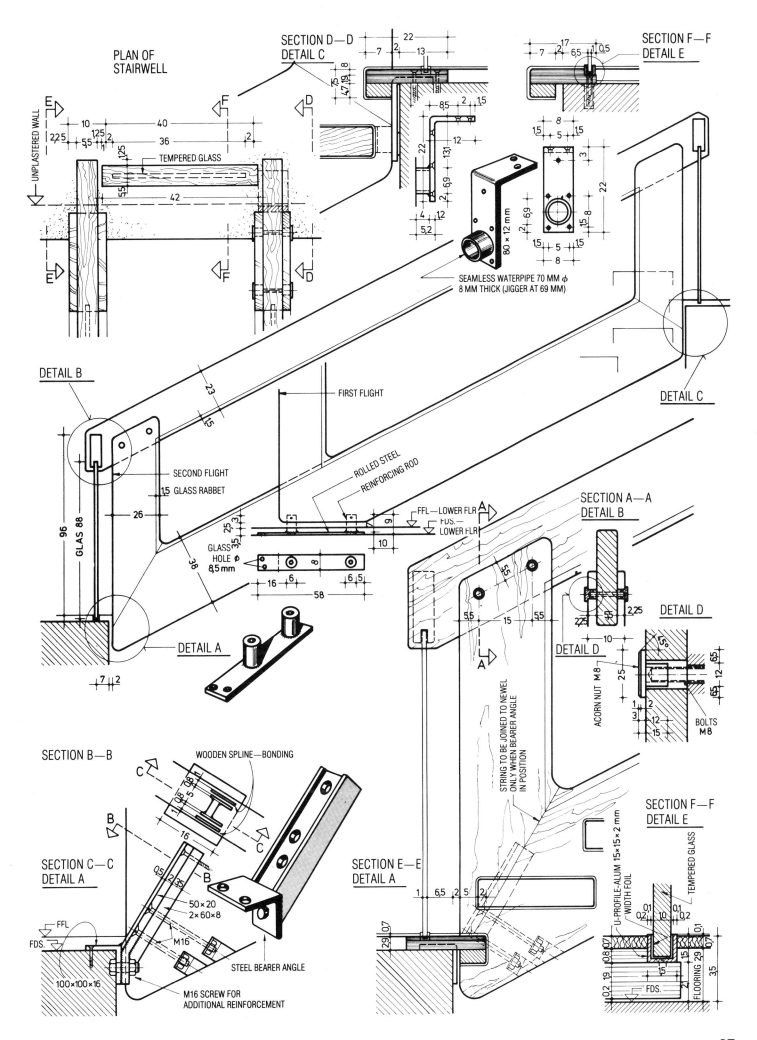

PLAN OF STAIRWELL

UNPLASTERED WALL

TEMPERED GLASS

SECTION D—D
DETAIL C

SEAMLESS WATERPIPE 70 MM ϕ
8 MM THICK (JIGGER AT 69 MM)

80 × 12 mm

SECTION F—F
DETAIL E

DETAIL B

DETAIL C

FIRST FLIGHT

SECOND FLIGHT

GLASS RABBET

ROLLED STEEL
REINFORCING ROD

GLAS 88

GLASS
HOLE ϕ
8,5 mm

DETAIL A

FFL—LOWER FLR
FDS.—
LOWER FLR

SECTION A—A
DETAIL B

DETAIL D

DETAIL D

ACORN NUT M8

BOLTS
M8

SECTION B—B

WOODEN SPLINE—BONDING

SECTION C—C
DETAIL A

FFL

FDS.

50 × 20
2 × 60 × 8

M16

100 × 100 × 16

STEEL BEARER ANGLE

M16 SCREW FOR
ADDITIONAL REINFORCEMENT

STRING TO BE JOINED TO NEWEL
ONLY WHEN BEARER ANGLE
IN POSITION

SECTION E—E
DETAIL A

SECTION F—F
DETAIL E

U-PROFILE-ALUM 15×15×2 mm
WIDTH FOIL

TEMPERED GLASS

FDS.

FLOORING

27

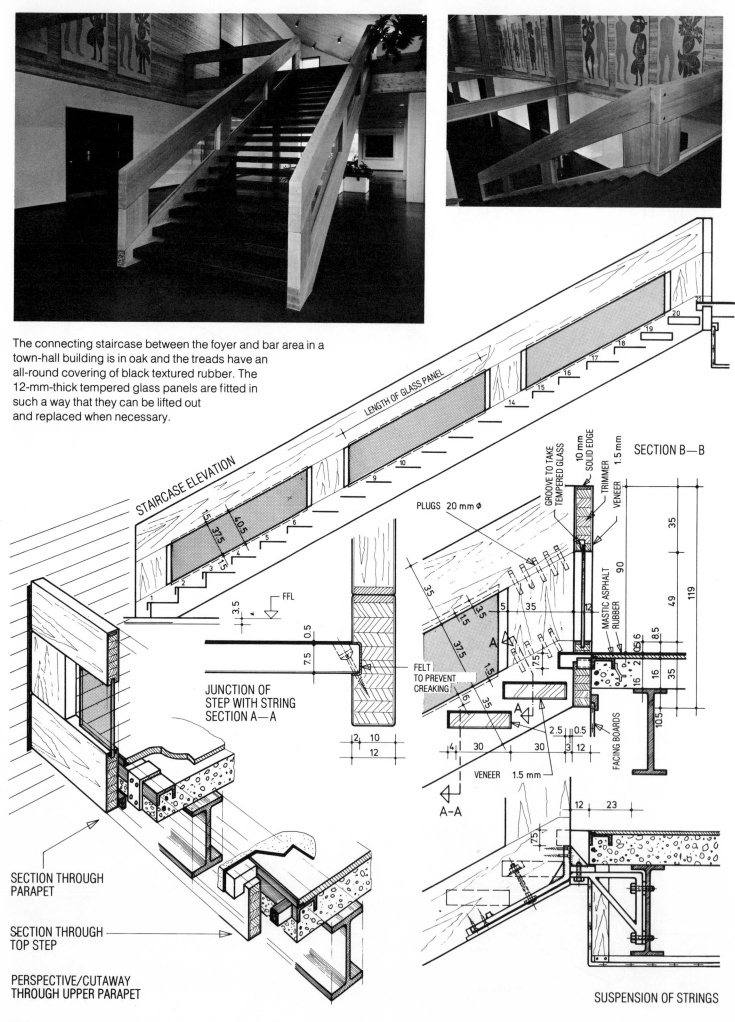

The connecting staircase between the foyer and bar area in a town-hall building is in oak and the treads have an all-round covering of black textured rubber. The 12-mm-thick tempered glass panels are fitted in such a way that they can be lifted out and replaced when necessary.

STAIRCASE ELEVATION

LENGTH OF GLASS PANEL

SECTION B—B

PLUGS 20 mm ∅

GROOVE TO TAKE TEMPERED GLASS

10 mm SOLID EDGE

TRIMMER

VENEER 1.5 mm

MASTIC ASPHALT RUBBER

FELT TO PREVENT CREAKING

FACING BOARDS

VENEER 1.5 mm

A—A

JUNCTION OF STEP WITH STRING SECTION A—A

FFL

SECTION THROUGH PARAPET

SECTION THROUGH TOP STEP

PERSPECTIVE/CUTAWAY THROUGH UPPER PARAPET

SUSPENSION OF STRINGS

This staircase is in a school; the wood used is mahogany and the surface and front edge of the treads have been lined with PVC. All timber sections are bonded. The laminae used in the treads have been saw-cut to a depth of 5 mm, which provides for more rapid drying of the glue.

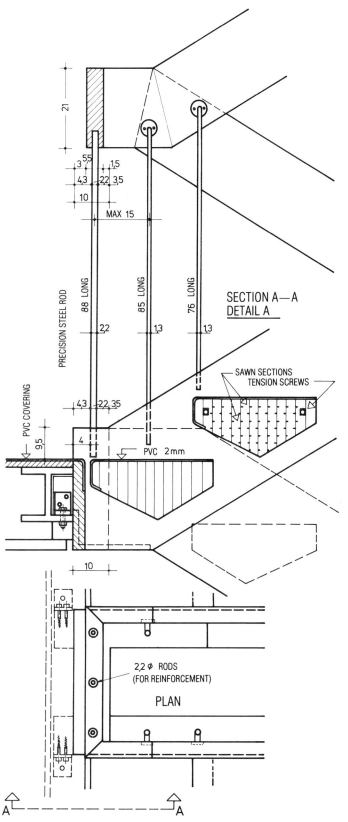

SECTION A—A
DETAIL A

PRECISION STEEL ROD

88 LONG

85 LONG

76 LONG

22

13

13

MAX 15

3 55 1,5
4,3 22 3,5
10

21

PVC COVERING

4,3 22 35

9,5

4

PVC 2 mm

SAWN SECTIONS
TENSION SCREWS

10

2,2 Ø RODS
(FOR REINFORCEMENT)

PLAN

A   A

The photograph on the far left shows a darkened oak staircase; the treads are covered with a yellow velour.

The open-riser stair in the right-hand photograph has infill panels of tempered glass.

The staircase in the illustration below has an interesting feature: a handrail held lightly in place by clearly visible screws.

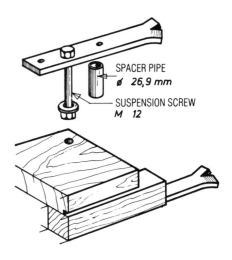

The stair shown above is partially supported on the open side; a highly individual and pleasing method of fixing to the wall has been used here.

The intersecting staircase shown in the four photographs below is based on a traditional method of construction. Sleeves have been sunk into the facing edges of the treads to hold the take-up bolts, which are finished with decorative nuts (the author's design); these are displayed deliberately. The handrail and guardrail are mitred on the turn to create a continuous, flowing line.

In the example below, the flight leads from the vestibule or hall to bedrooms situated in the basement; from the living room, another flight leads up into the attic.

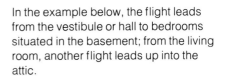

At the top left is a staircase whose pine strings are recessed on both sides to take the darkened oak treads; the handrail is also darkened oak. The stair at the top right has laminated timber strings; light oak has been chosen for the treads, handrail, and guardrail. In the two staircases illustrated at the bottom, the treads are mounted on wooden brackets.

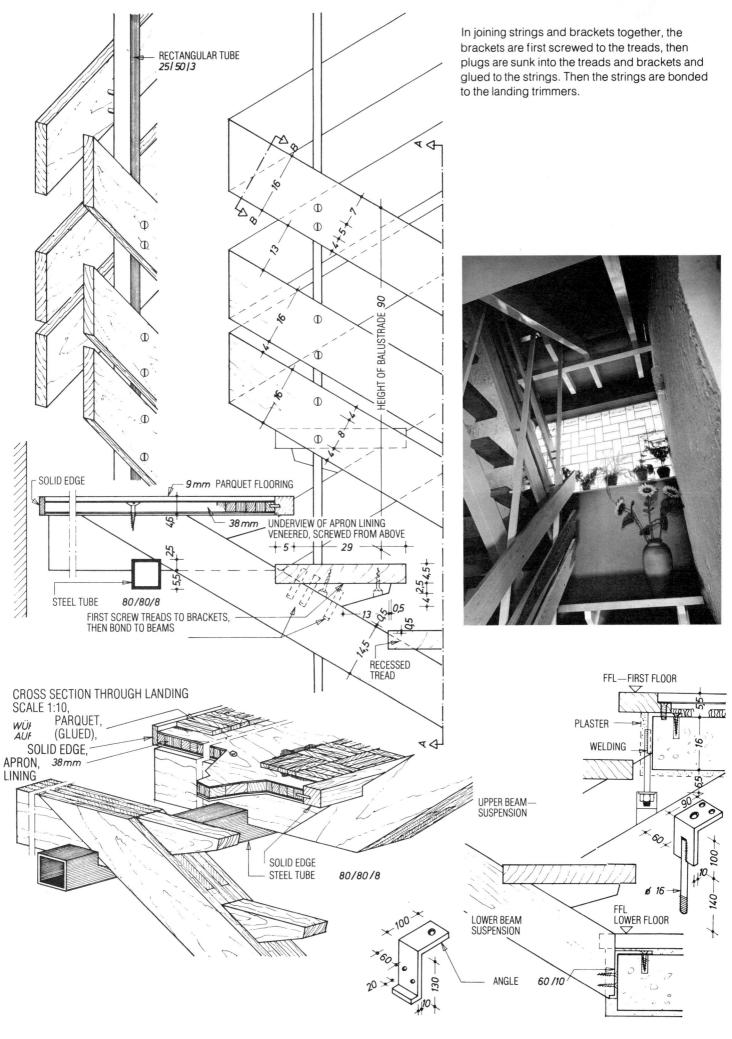

RECTANGULAR TUBE
25/50/3

In joining strings and brackets together, the brackets are first screwed to the treads, then plugs are sunk into the treads and brackets and glued to the strings. Then the strings are bonded to the landing trimmers.

B

B

A

16

13

16

15

4 + 5 + 7

16

8 + 4

HEIGHT OF BALUSTRADE 90

SOLID EDGE

9 mm PARQUET FLOORING

4,5

38 mm

UNDERVIEW OF APRON LINING
VENEERED, SCREWED FROM ABOVE

5

29

STEEL TUBE 80/80/8

25

5,5

2,5 4,5

13 0,5 0,5

0,5

14,5

FIRST SCREW TREADS TO BRACKETS,
THEN BOND TO BEAMS

RECESSED
TREAD

A

CROSS SECTION THROUGH LANDING
SCALE 1:10,

WÜI
AUF

PARQUET,
(GLUED),
SOLID EDGE,

APRON, 38mm
LINING

SOLID EDGE
STEEL TUBE 80/80/8

UPPER BEAM—
SUSPENSION

LOWER BEAM
SUSPENSION

ANGLE 60/10

FFL—FIRST FLOOR

PLASTER

WELDING

5,5

16

6,5

90

60

10

100

ø 16

140

FFL
LOWER FLOOR

100

60

130

20

10

33

Here the connection of the balusters to the floor is particularly practical: threaded bolts are plugged into the floor and both concrete and wooden steps, and tube sockets are sunk into the facings of the baluster boards. The underside of the stairs and the treads and risers are carpeted and, finally, the balusters are screwed in position and the balustrade installed.

This connecting stair is made entirely of oak; the chrome balusters lend it an elegant appearance.

Strings and handrails are in rough knotted pine and this provides continuity between the laminated timber beams in the upstairs ceiling and the cladding used elsewhere. The treads are oak and the floor covering is burnt bricks. Each laminated step is plugged to the recessed strings in four places. The top steps run across the entire width of the stairwell and are anchored directly to the concrete platforms by steel bearer angles. The strings are mounted on welded steel angles.

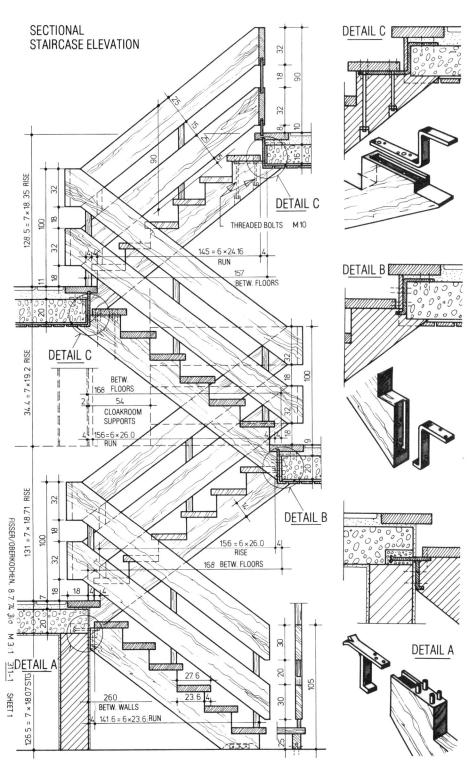

SECTIONAL STAIRCASE ELEVATION

DETAIL C

THREADED BOLTS M 10

DETAIL B

DETAIL A

Various types of straight-flight string stairs

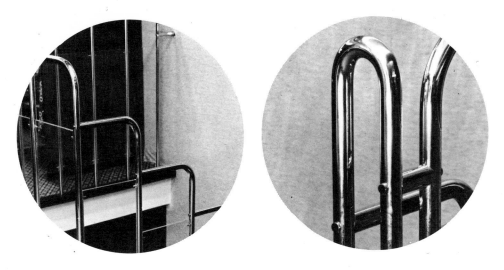

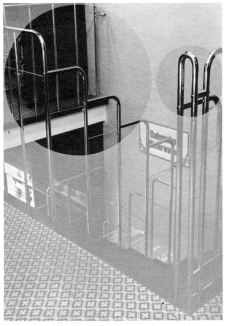

Shown in the illustrations on this and the following page is a typical connecting stair in a boutique. The laminated spine string, which has been painted white, creates an interesting appearance in this staircase when contrasted with the laminated darkened oak steps. The integration of treads and risers means that the stair is absolutely resistant to warping. Chromed-steel border tubes, bolted in position, frame 12-mm-thick Plexiglas panels.

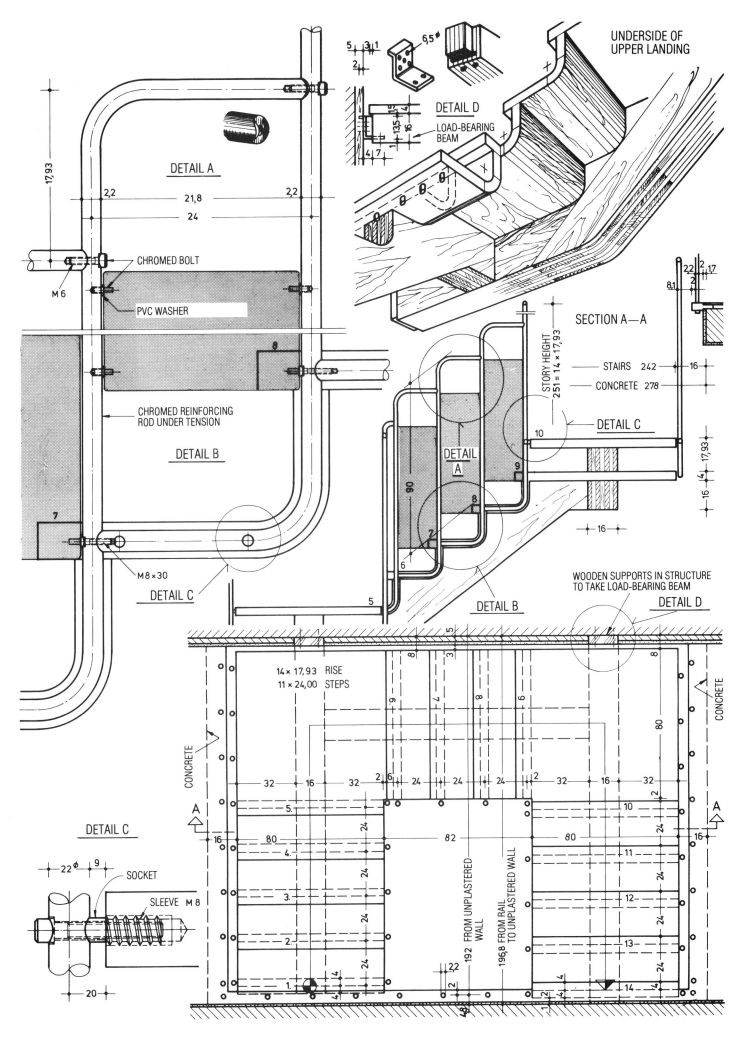

DETAIL A

17,93

2,2   21,8   2,2
24

CHROMED BOLT

M 6

PVC WASHER

CHROMED REINFORCING
ROD UNDER TENSION

DETAIL B

8

7

M 8×30

DETAIL C

5   3   1
2
6,5⌀

DETAIL D

LOAD-BEARING
BEAM

135
16
4   7

UNDERSIDE OF
UPPER LANDING

22   2   17
2
8,1

SECTION A—A

STAIRS   242   16

CONCRETE   278

DETAIL C

10

9

17,93

16

16

STORY HEIGHT
251 = 14 × 17,93

90

DETAIL
A

8

6

DETAIL B

WOODEN SUPPORTS IN STRUCTURE
TO TAKE LOAD-BEARING BEAM

DETAIL D

5

5

8   3   8   6   8

9   7   8   6

CONCRETE

80

CONCRETE

14 × 17,93   RISE
11 × 24,00   STEPS

32   16   32   2 6   24   24   24   2   32   16   32

2

A   A

5.   10

16   16

80   82   80

4.   11

3.   12

2.   13

24   24   24   24   24   24

192 FROM UNPLASTERED WALL

196,8 FROM RAIL TO UNPLASTERED WALL

22
2

1.   14

4

2

DETAIL C

22⌀   9

SOCKET

SLEEVE M 8

20

39

This staircase runs through several stories in an office building. The parapets on each floor are beech-veneered blockboard, to which solid-wood quarter wreaths have been affixed. The semicircular guardrails at the turns of the half-landings are made of formed veneer. The handrails comprise 30-mm-thick L-shaped, bonded beech boards; these are joined to the chromed-steel structure. Tempered glass panels, 12 mm thick, are fixed between the supporting steel banister rods. All the wooden parts of this staircase have been stained scarlet-red and then sealed.

Department store stair with landing:

1. Steel support beam
2. Steel tread
3. Welding seam
4. Layer of 22-mm blockboard
5. Plywood trimmer plate, 6 mm
6. Layer of carpet
7. PVC edge strip
8. 12-mm tempered glass
9. Grip fillet
10. Fawn-colored imitation leather trim
11. Mitred imitation leather
12. Blockboard handrail
13. Hardwood edges
14. Chromed-steel housing
15. Chromed-steel tube
16. Chrome base plate
17. Welded cleats
18. Plugged wooden base plate, plastic-coated

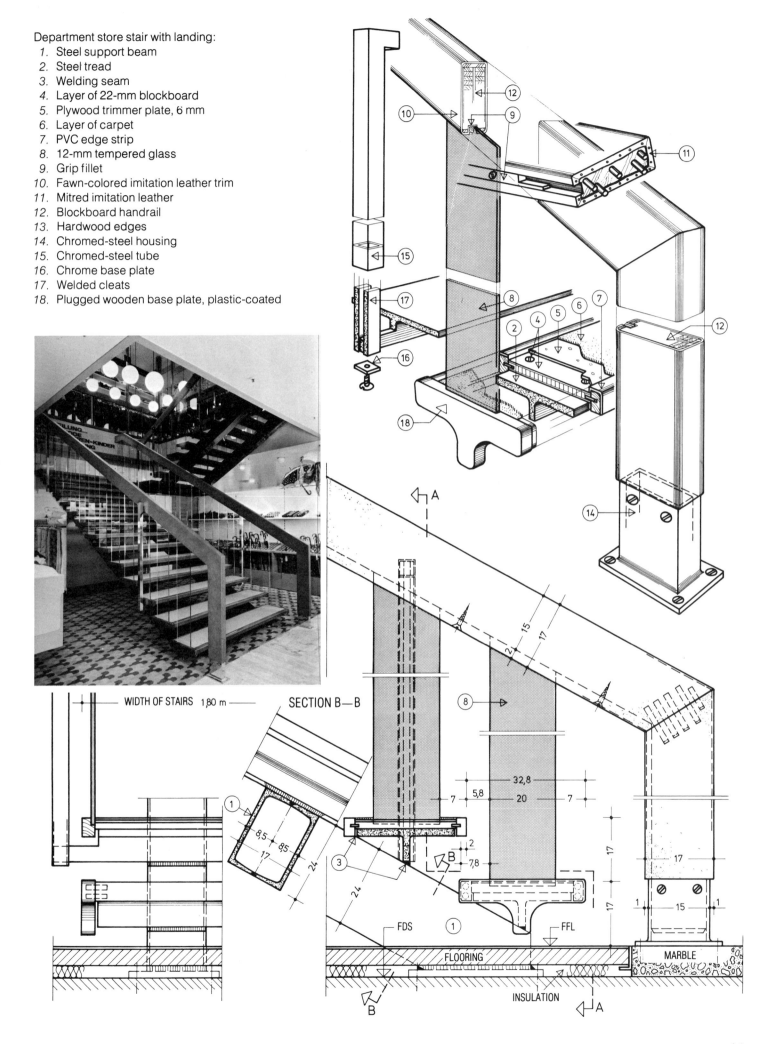

WIDTH OF STAIRS 1,80 m

SECTION B—B

FDS

FFL

FLOORING

MARBLE

INSULATION

In this balustrade, solid mahogany has been stained reddish brown and given a mat silk finish. The bearer angles for the lower edge of the balustrade should be fastened with dowels before the steps are mounted. Since the mitres cannot be cut before installation, this is a case where the necessary surface treatment cannot be carried out until the balustrade is fixed in position.

VARIATIONS ON CLOSED STAIRWELLS

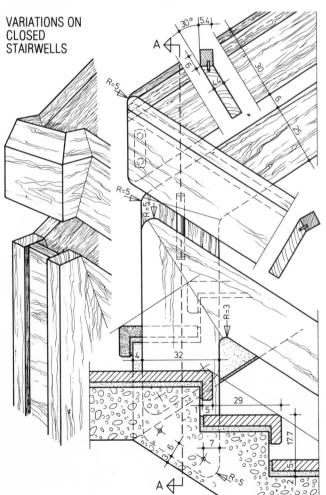

SECTION A—A

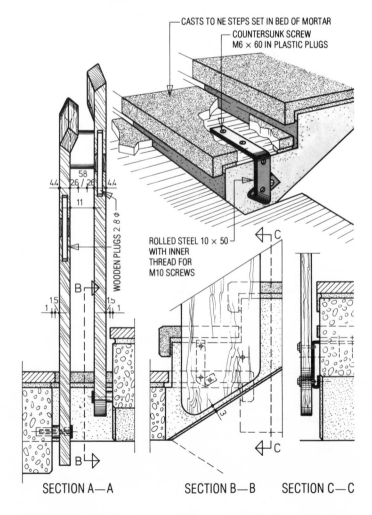

CASTS TO NE STEPS SET IN BED OF MORTAR
COUNTERSUNK SCREW M6 × 60 IN PLASTIC PLUGS

ROLLED STEEL 10 × 50 WITH INNER THREAD FOR M10 SCREWS

WOODEN PLUGS 2.8 ∅

SECTION B—B   SECTION C—C

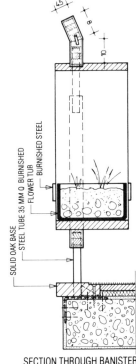

SECTION THROUGH BANISTER
WITH FLOWER BOX

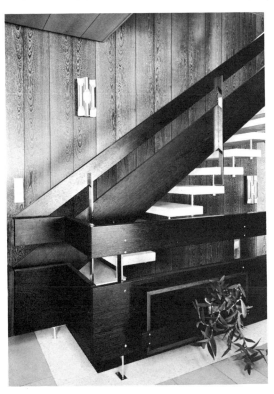

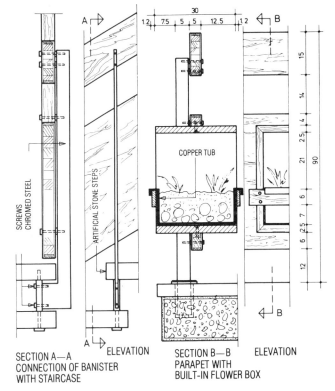

SCREWS
CHROMED STEEL

ARTIFICIAL STONE STEPS

COPPER TUB

SECTION A—A
CONNECTION OF BANISTER
WITH STAIRCASE

ELEVATION

SECTION B—B
PARAPET WITH
BUILT-IN FLOWER BOX

ELEVATION

Long stretches of balustrade can be
visually broken up for a good effect
by installing flower boxes.

6.2 Straight and rectangular stairs with suspended or supported treads

6.2.1 Treads suspended on or supported by steel rods

This open-riser, dog-leg staircase exhibits a construction where the treads are supported on one side by steel rods. The stair has four flights and landings and spans two stories. The wall strings are of larch and the treads of solid beech. Detail A shows the metal core rail which travels through the center of the construction. The fixing of the handrails gives extra stability to the steel rods.

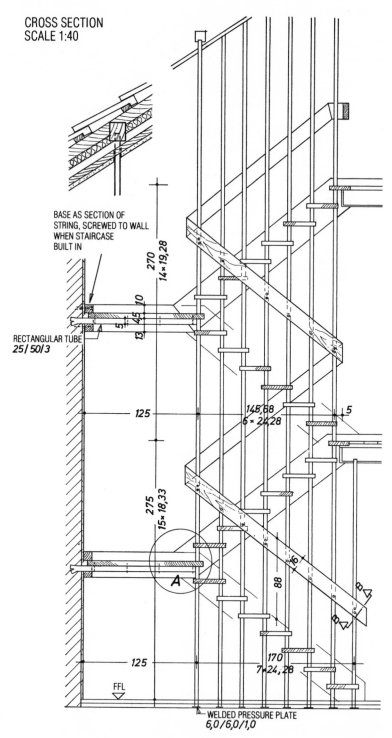

CROSS SECTION
SCALE 1:40

BASE AS SECTION OF
STRING, SCREWED TO WALL
WHEN STAIRCASE
BUILT IN

RECTANGULAR TUBE
25 / 50 / 3

270
14 × 19,28

10
5
45
13

125

275
15 × 18,33

145,68
6 × 24,28

5

88

A

125

170
7 × 24,28

FFL

WELDED PRESSURE PLATE
6,0 / 6,0 / 1,0

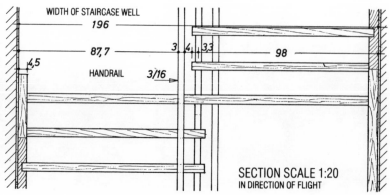

WIDTH OF STAIRCASE WELL
196

87,7

4,5

HANDRAIL

3 4 3,3

98

3/16

SECTION SCALE 1:20
IN DIRECTION OF FLIGHT

In this open and airy stair, the curve of the handrail is reminiscent of the shape of a gazelle or springbok in flight. There is a tendency to buckle at both abutments, but this is counteracted by sinking approximately eight dowels at each point. The 22-mm-thick steel rods, each running through two steps, also prevent the possibility of the handrail buckling. When the staircase is installed, both treads and rods are drilled and then bolted together.

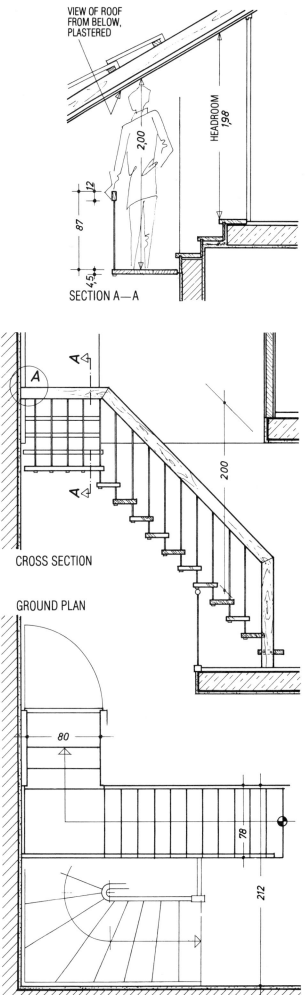

VIEW OF ROOF FROM BELOW, PLASTERED

HEADROOM 1,98

2,00

87

12

4,5

SECTION A—A

CROSS SECTION

200

GROUND PLAN

80

78

212

6.2.2 Treads supported by steel rods

The steel rods must be fixed to the horizontal banister boards, to the top step which spans the width of the stairwell, and to the treads themselves in order to prevent buckling.

On the ground floor (far left), a flower box at the turn of the stair makes an attractive infill. On the flight leading to the upper floor (near left), the rods are attached to the underside of the handrail, while the top steps are actually suspended from the handrail.

In order to give this steep staircase a lighter and more graceful appearance, only every second suspension rod meets the handrail. This dog-leg, half-helical stair is only 1.70 m wide. Suspension rods are used here so that as much light as possible can pass through into the living area.

Here, the lower two handrail supports have a secondary function: they support the load-bearing guardrail so that it does not buckle inwards. Only every second tread is suspended on the outer side. Flower boxes break the line of the upper parapet in a most attractive way.

Two new staircases of very narrow proportions had to be built during the renovation of an old building. The steel core rod, which has been painted white, serves to anchor the handrail and support the bottom few treads. The remaining treads are suspended on chrome rods. Each tread is connected to the wall by two 8 x 80 lag screws. Plastic dowels have been sunk into the facings of the treads.

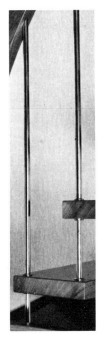

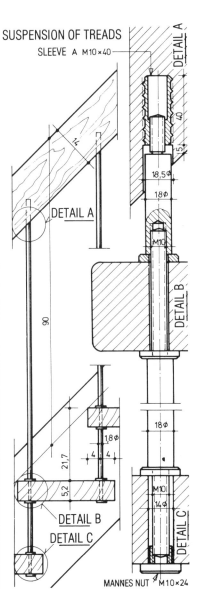

SUSPENSION OF TREADS
SLEEVE A M10×40
DETAIL A
DETAIL A
DETAIL B
DETAIL C
DETAIL B
DETAIL C
MANNES NUT M10×24

The particular characteristics of this open-riser stair are the suspended treads. To prevent these from swinging, the wall string is anchored twice to the wall at the points of connection. The guardrail on the outer side can be supported if necessary at its lower section by a chrome rod. The treads are laminated and are therefore warp-free. The guardrail and handrail are both made of darkened oak, laterally veneered with marsh oak. The installation of flower boxes in the parapet in the living room makes a pleasing visual break.

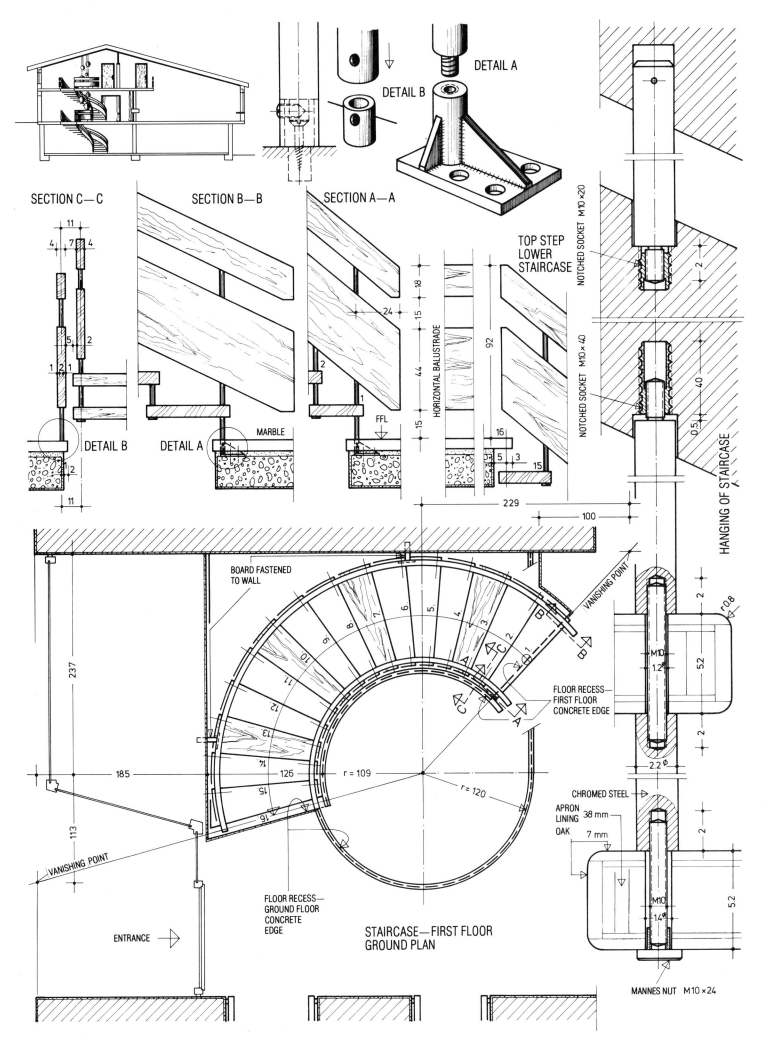

DETAIL B

DETAIL A

SECTION C—C

SECTION B—B

SECTION A—A

TOP STEP
LOWER
STAIRCASE

DETAIL B

DETAIL A

MARBLE

FFL

HORIZONTAL BALUSTRADE

NOTCHED SOCKET M10×20

NOTCHED SOCKET M10×40

HANGING OF STAIRCASE

229

100

BOARD FASTENED
TO WALL

VANISHING POINT

FLOOR RECESS—
FIRST FLOOR
CONCRETE EDGE

237

185

126

r = 109

r = 120

113

VANISHING POINT

ENTRANCE

FLOOR RECESS—
GROUND FLOOR
CONCRETE
EDGE

STAIRCASE—FIRST FLOOR
GROUND PLAN

CHROMED STEEL

APRON
LINING
OAK

38 mm

7 mm

M10
1.2

2.2 ∅

r 0.8

5.2

MANNES NUT M10×24

M10
1.4

5.2

49

In order to shorten the load-bearing length of the handrail, this one (above and right) is anchored to the concrete floor.

The laminated treads shown below are anchored firmly to the concrete floor above by suspension rods that have been extended as far up as the handrails.

6.2.3 Treads mortised into baluster boards

Illustrated below is a stair with landing which has an L-shaped handrail. Each part of the staircase is laminated.

The treads have been sunk with sockets into which threaded bolts have been screwed. These are capped with nuts designed by the author.

Both bottom illustrations show a stair where a handrail has been added on the wall side.

This slab stair with landing forms an integrated unit with the upper parapet, shelf unit, and eating area. Since the balustrade acts as a rigid surface, only laminated materials can be used. Each tread is constructed from two 22-mm-thick blockboards that are bonded together.

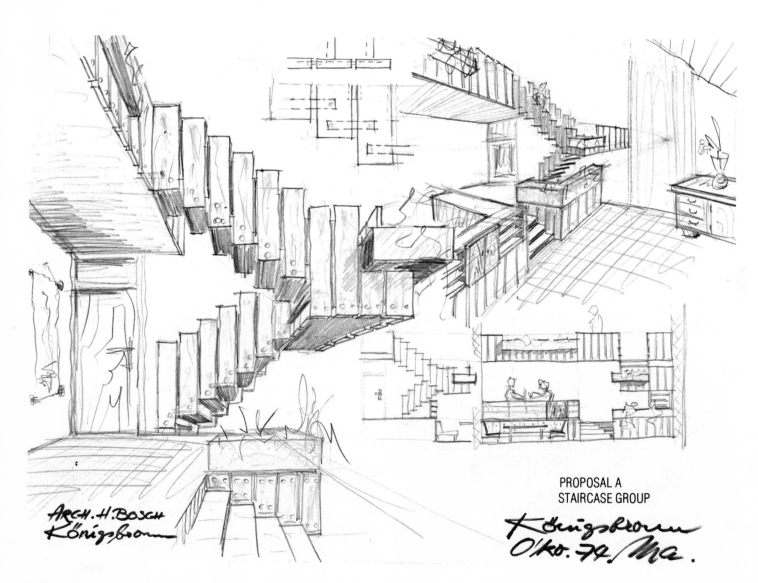

ARCH. H. BOSCH
Königsbronn

PROPOSAL A
STAIRCASE GROUP

Königsbronn
O'Ko. 79/Ma.

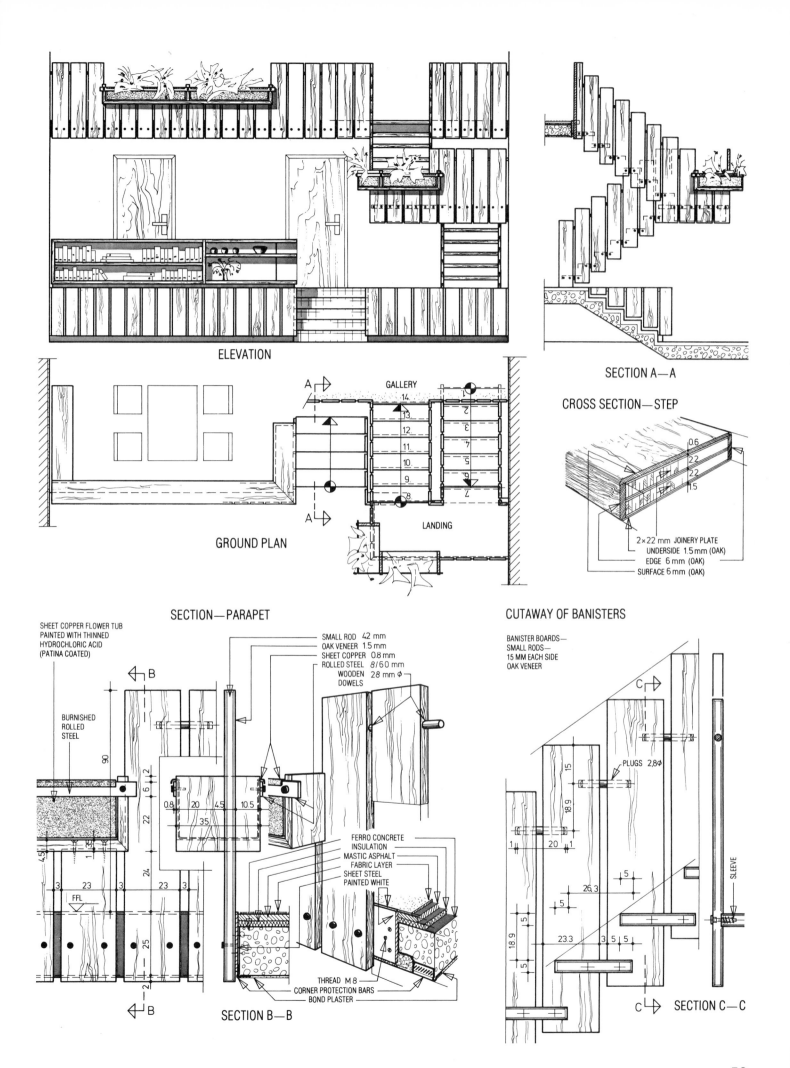

ELEVATION

GROUND PLAN

SECTION A—A

CROSS SECTION—STEP

GALLERY

14
13
12
11
10
9
8

LANDING

1
2
3
4
5
6
7

0.6
22
22
15

2×22 mm JOINERY PLATE
UNDERSIDE 1.5 mm (OAK)
EDGE 6 mm (OAK)
SURFACE 6 mm (OAK)

SECTION—PARAPET

CUTAWAY OF BANISTERS

SHEET COPPER FLOWER TUB
PAINTED WITH THINNED
HYDROCHLORIC ACID
(PATINA COATED)

BURNISHED
ROLLED
STEEL

SMALL ROD   42 mm
OAK VENEER 1.5 mm
SHEET COPPER 0.8 mm
ROLLED STEEL 8/60 mm
WOODEN
DOWELS 28 mm Ø

BANISTER BOARDS—
SMALL RODS—
15 MM EACH SIDE
OAK VENEER

FERRO CONCRETE
INSULATION
MASTIC ASPHALT
FABRIC LAYER
SHEET STEEL
PAINTED WHITE

PLUGS 2,8Ø

SLEEVE

90
12
6
22
24
0.8
20
4.5
10.5
35
4.5
1
3   23   3   24   23   3
FFL
25
2

THREAD M 8
CORNER PROTECTION BARS
BOND PLASTER

SECTION B—B

15
18.9
1   20   1
5
26.3
5
18.9   23.3   3 5 5
5

SECTION C—C

53

6.2.4 Space-saving straight-flight stairs

If conventional treads are used in this type of stair, only the back part of the foot is able to touch the step when descending (*1*), and the front edge of the step above tends to hit the calf (*2*). The steps illustrated in sketch *2* make descent much easier by having sections cut away, as shown. The disadvantage in the implementation of this solution is that it is always necessary to start off with the same foot when climbing. Sketch *4* offers two further possibilities for the arrangement of treads.

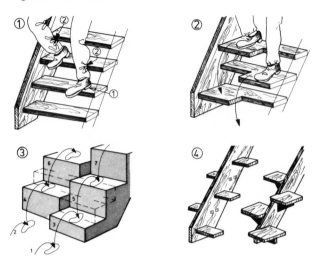

Since space-saving stairs must be installed at a very steep angle, they should be used only in those parts of the house where strangers would not normally be expected to use them. The contractor should note the advantages and disadvantages of this type of stair.

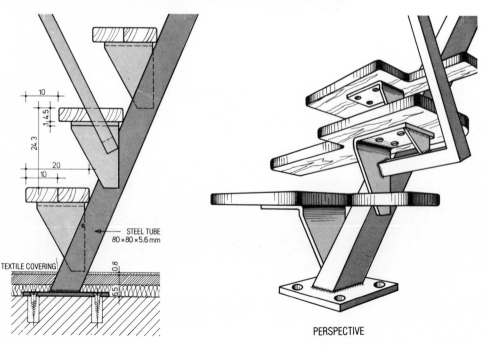

PERSPECTIVE

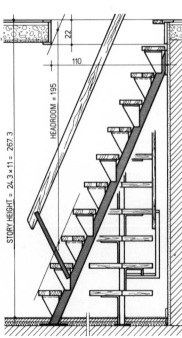

6.3 Spiral (helical) staircases

6.3.1 Examples of design

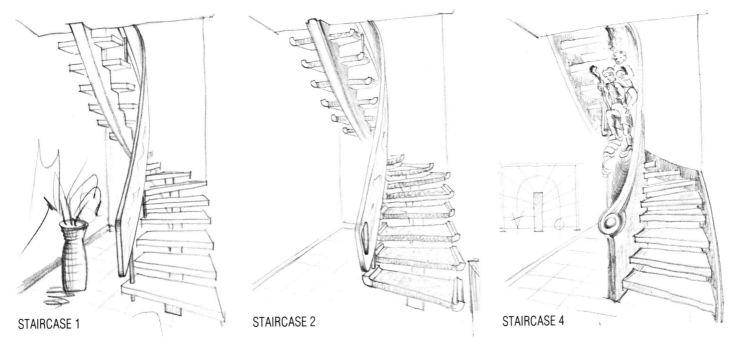

STAIRCASE 1
STAIRCASE 2
STAIRCASE 4

6.3.2 Spiral (helical) string stairs

Newel posts, handrails, and strings are united into one flowing element by the use of heat-molded Plexiglas infill panels. A thin fillet of felt between the Plexiglas and the groove cut in the wood to take it prevents squeaking when the stair is in service. It should be noted that Plexiglas contracts when curved.

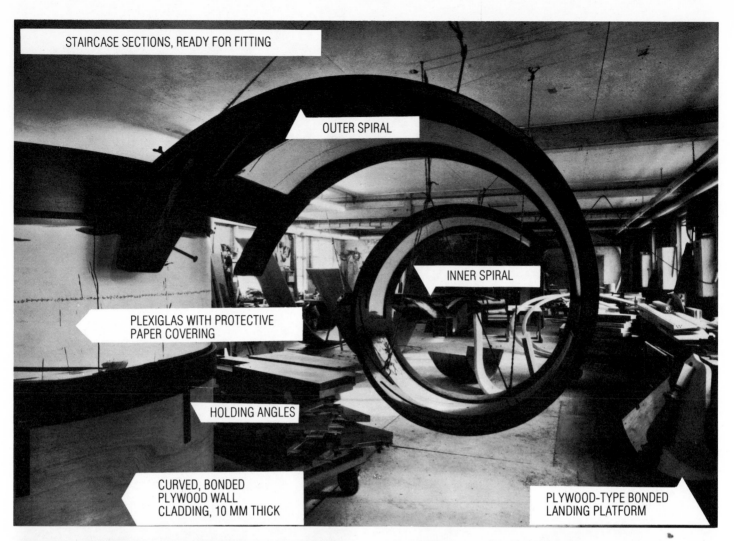

STAIRCASE SECTIONS, READY FOR FITTING

OUTER SPIRAL

INNER SPIRAL

PLEXIGLAS WITH PROTECTIVE PAPER COVERING

HOLDING ANGLES

CURVED, BONDED PLYWOOD WALL CLADDING, 10 MM THICK

PLYWOOD-TYPE BONDED LANDING PLATFORM

A rounding of all edges has been achieved in this connecting stair by keeping strings, handrails, and newel posts the same thickness.

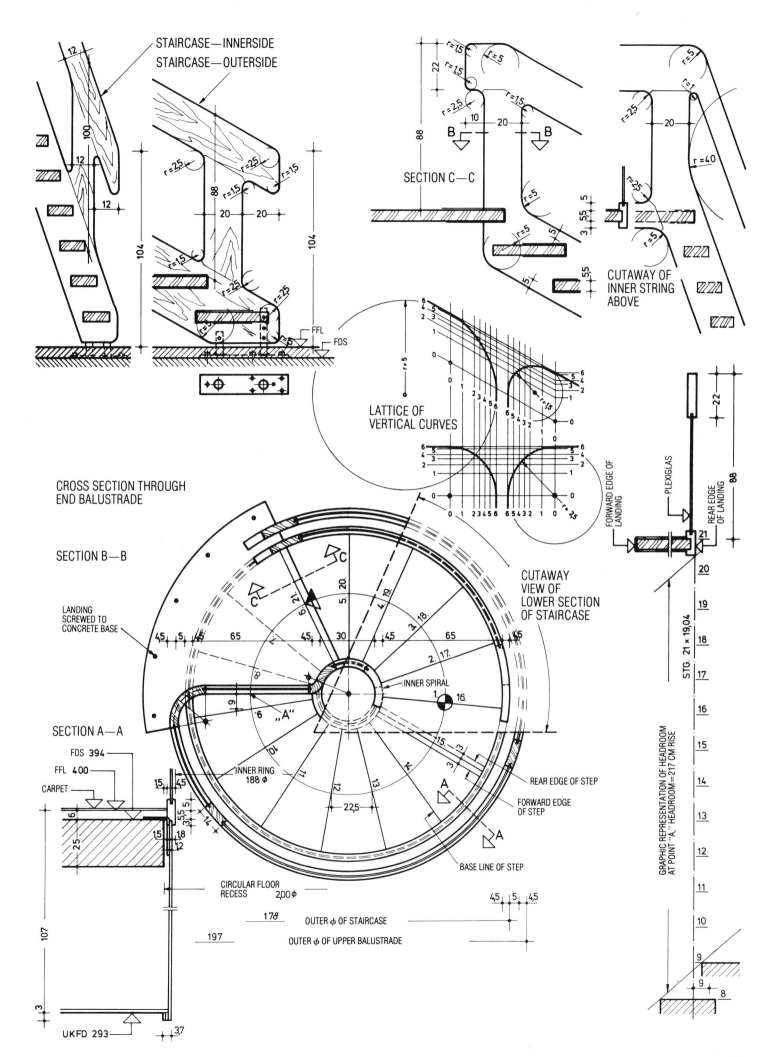

STAIRCASE—INNERSIDE
STAIRCASE—OUTERSIDE

SECTION C—C

CUTAWAY OF
INNER STRING
ABOVE

LATTICE OF
VERTICAL CURVES

FORWARD EDGE OF
LANDING

CROSS SECTION THROUGH
END BALUSTRADE

SECTION B—B

CUTAWAY
VIEW OF
LOWER SECTION
OF STAIRCASE

LANDING
SCREWED TO
CONCRETE BASE

PLEXIGLAS

FORWARD EDGE OF
LANDING

REAR EDGE
OF LANDING

SECTION A—A

FDS 394
FFL 400
CARPET

INNER SPIRAL

INNER RING
188 ⌀

REAR EDGE OF STEP

FORWARD EDGE
OF STEP

BASE LINE OF STEP

CIRCULAR FLOOR
RECESS   200 ⌀

178   OUTER ⌀ OF STAIRCASE

197   OUTER ⌀ OF UPPER BALUSTRADE

UKFD 293

STG. 21 × 19,04

GRAPHIC REPRESENTATION OF HEADROOM
AT POINT "A," HEADROOM=217 CM RISE

59

The simplicity of this stair, with an emphasis on line, complements the style of the house in which it is situated. It has been precast and has a carpet covering. An interesting feature is the way in which the same carpet is continued on to the wall at the points where the steps connect, with brass strips affording protection to the edges of the carpet where it meets the plastered wall. On the open side of the stair, the laminated timber string has been fixed to the rim of the concrete wall with concealed screws. Ten-mm-thick heat-molded Plexiglas is used to provide infill panels for the balustrade. Note how skillfully the junction of the landing slab, top step, and parapet is executed, and how it is totally in keeping with the design of the stair.

The wall cladding and balusters in this staircase are veneered in stone pine and the treads are laminated oak; these are held in place by brass fillister-head screws and sockets.

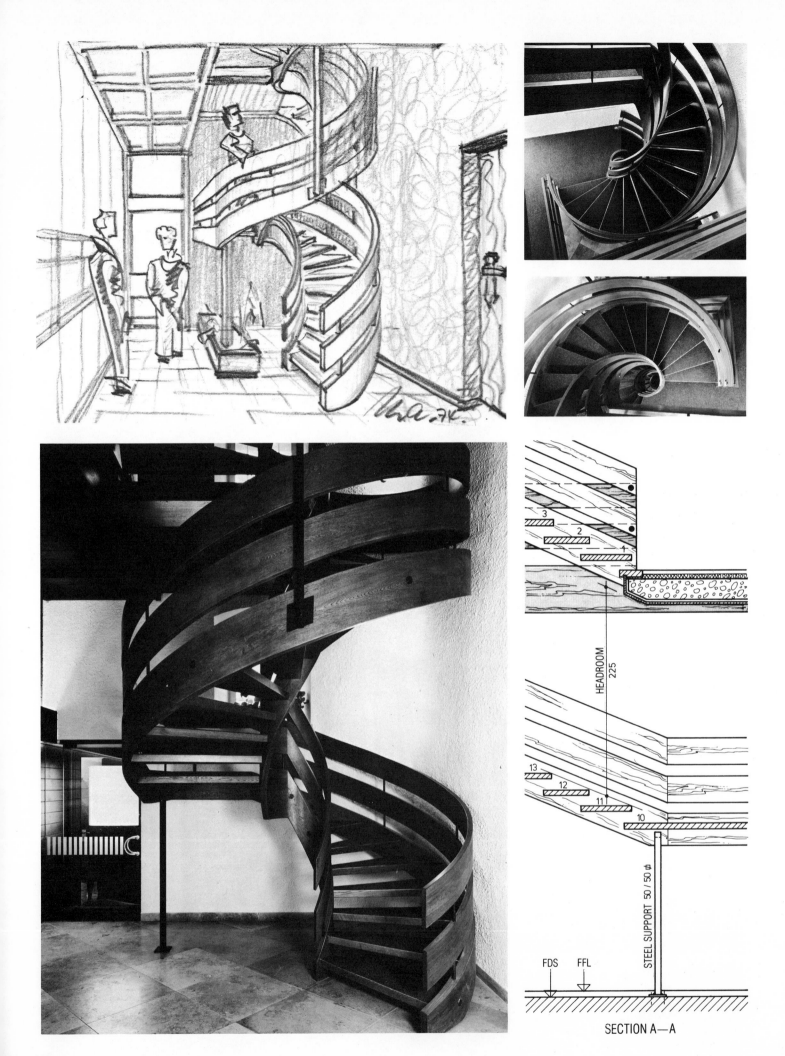

HEADROOM
225

3
2

13
12
11
10

STEEL SUPPORT 50 / 50 ⌀

FDS   FFL

SECTION A—A

The requirements for this semihelical staircase with a quarter-space landing built-in, which leads up from a restaurant to clubrooms above, were that it should have a timeless, classic design and also be comfortable to use. Both examples illustrated below show the traverse from the lower to the upper stair. The first solution shows the use of rounded wreath portions at the open side and the outer side of the stair between the outer string and the parapet. An alternative is to bring the outer string and the parapet so far forward that the points of intersection occur at a balustrade height of 90 cm. This latter solution is more attractive but, since it reduces the clear width from 1.55 m to 1.25 m, it is not to be recommended. A further possibility is to set the upper stair further back, but this would shorten the walkline and make the stair steeper.

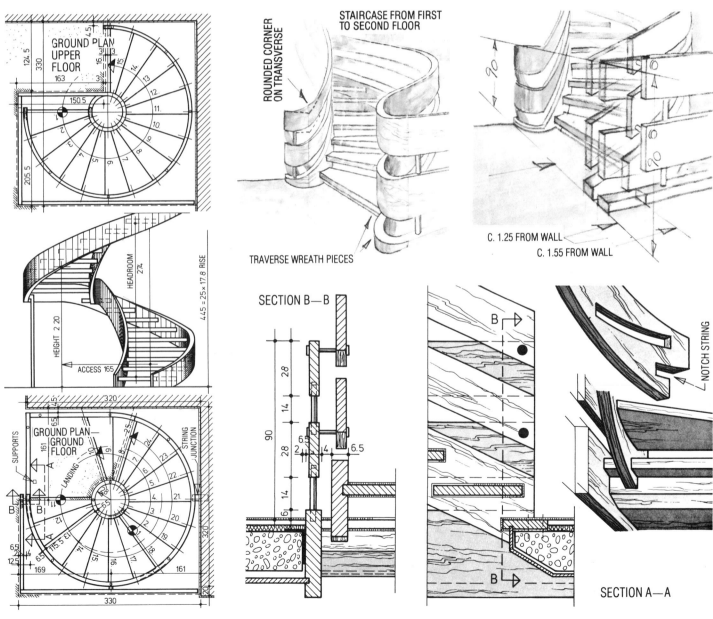

Manufacturing the strings for this open-riser stair proved to be exceptionally difficult, since 3-mm pine veneers had to be bonded in sections to form a curved laminated surface with a final thickness of 8 cm. Ten-cm-thick tempered glass panels are used as infills for the parapets. The treads are darkened oak.

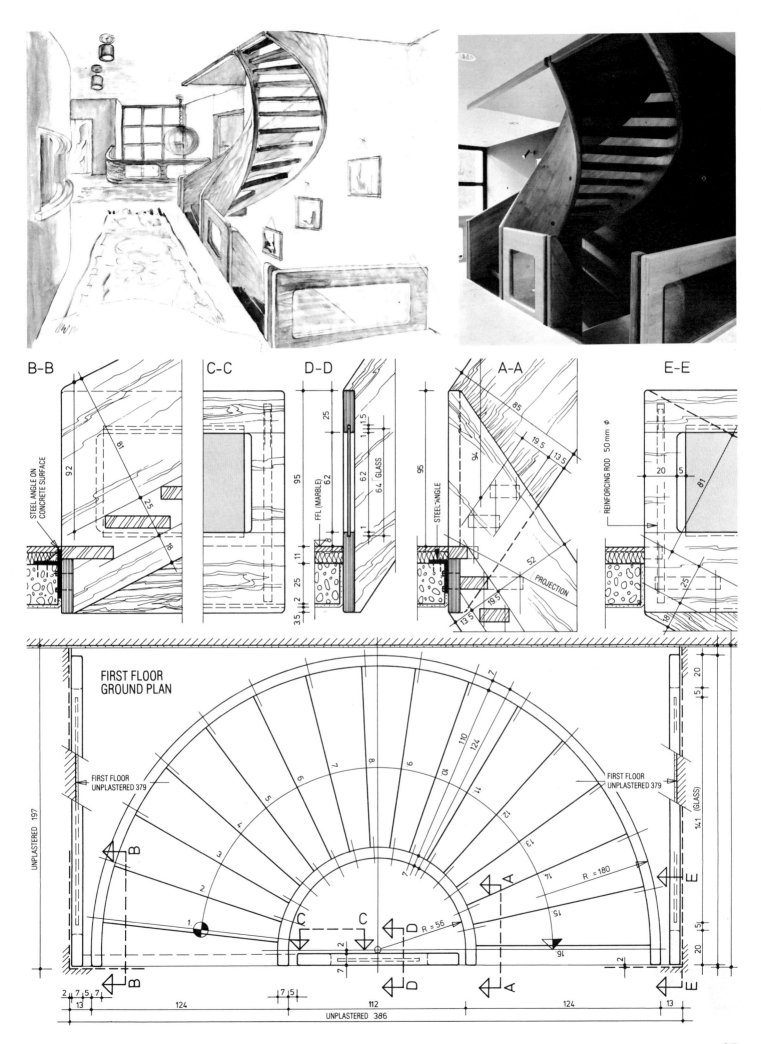

B-B

STEEL ANGLE ON CONCRETE SURFACE

92
81
25
18

C-C

D-D

25
95
1 1.5
62
62 GLASS
64
FFL (MARBLE)
8
11
1
3.5 2 25

A-A

85
94
95
19 5
13 5
STEEL ANGLE
52
PROJECTION
13 5 19 5

E-E

REINFORCING ROD 50 mm ø
20 5
81
25
18

FIRST FLOOR
GROUND PLAN

FIRST FLOOR
UNPLASTERED 379

FIRST FLOOR
UNPLASTERED 379

UNPLASTERED 197

7
110
124
8
6
9
Ø10
5
11
4
12
3
13
2
14
R = 180
1
15
R = 56
16

14 1 (GLASS)

5 20

5

20

2

B

B

C C

D D

A A

E

E

2 7 5 7
13
7 5
124
112
124
13

UNPLASTERED 386

65

The central support elements of the staircase on this page are laminated 5-cm-thick boards. A rustic effect is achieved through the choice of a rough carpet layer and the wrought iron brackets, through which a hemp cord is threaded.

Shown on the facing page is a half-helical stair; its central support element acts as a framework. Since the space available for the construction of this staircase is very narrow, no stairwell (i.e., the open space between two outer strings) is present. Instead, the outer string is developed as a framework and fitted with tempered glass panels. A pleasant color blend is achieved by the choice of a light green carpet and of floor tiles with a pattern of light and dark green. The oak chosen for the staircase also provides a good contrast with the rustic burnt brick wall. The handrail, which has not yet been positioned, is made from polished V-2a steel.

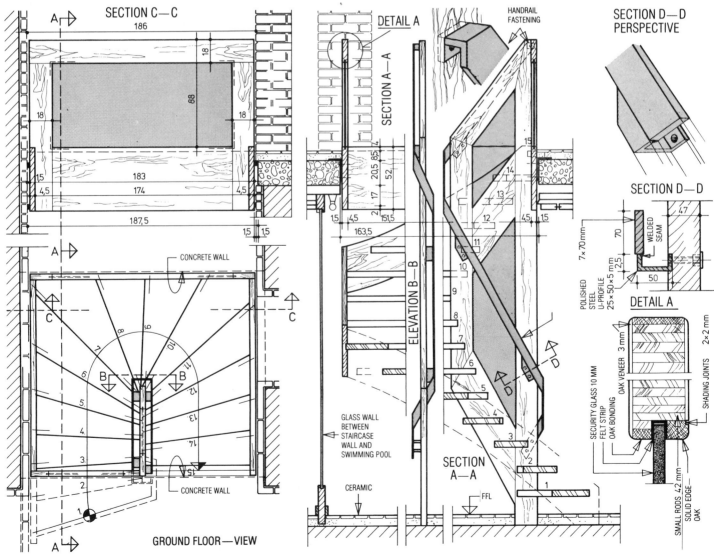

SECTION C—C

186

18

88

18 18

15

183

174

4,5 4,5

187,5

1,5 1,5

A—A

CONCRETE WALL

C — C

B — B

CONCRETE WALL

GROUND FLOOR—VIEW

DETAIL A

HANDRAIL FASTENING

SECTION A—A

20,5 85

52

17

1,5 4,5

2

151,5

163,5

GLASS WALL
BETWEEN
STAIRCASE
WALL AND
SWIMMING POOL

CERAMIC

ELEVATION B—B

15

14

13

12

11

10

9

8

7

6

5

4

3

2

1

45 15

**SECTION
A—A**

FFL

SECTION D—D
PERSPECTIVE

SECTION D—D

47

70

2,5

WELDED
SEAM

50

POLISHED
STEEL
U-PROFILE
25×50×5 mm

7×70mm

DETAIL A

2×2 mm

SECURITY GLASS 10 MM

FELT STRIP

OAK BONDING

OAK VENEER 3 mm

SHADING JOINTS

SMALL RODS 4,2 mm

SOLID EDGE
OAK

67

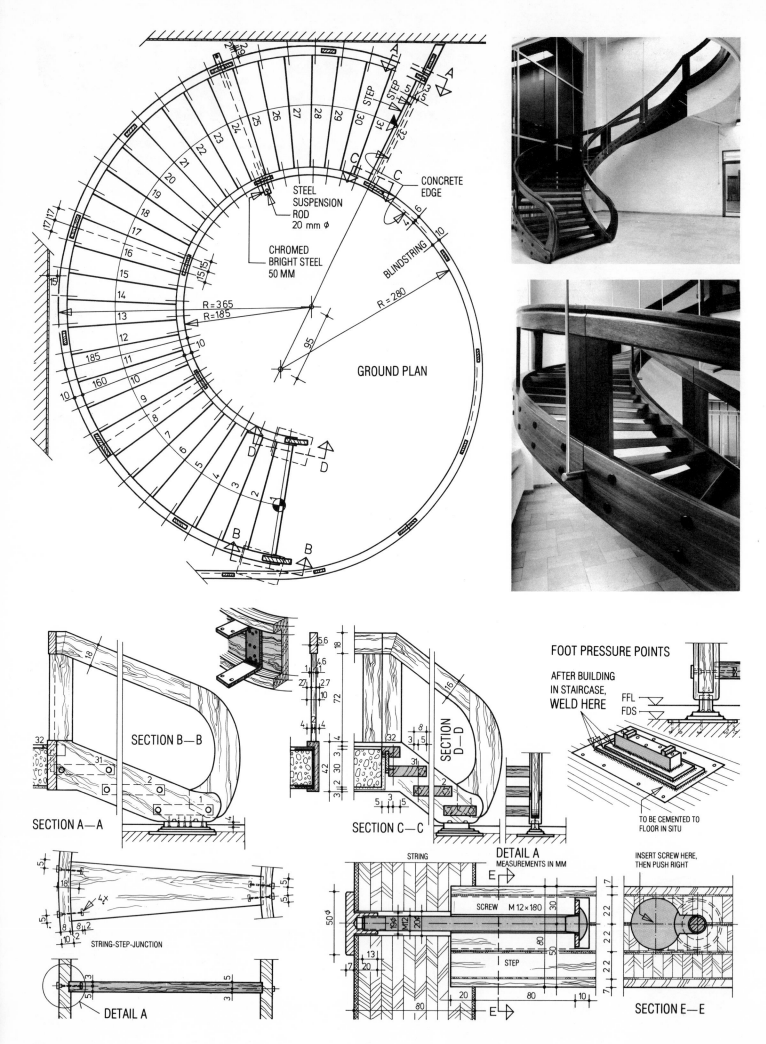

GROUND PLAN

STEEL
SUSPENSION
ROD
20 mm ⌀

CHROMED
BRIGHT STEEL
50 MM

CONCRETE
EDGE

BLINDSTRING

R = 365
R = 185
R = 280
95

STEP

SECTION B—B

SECTION A—A

STRING-STEP-JUNCTION

DETAIL A

SECTION C—C

SECTION D—D

DETAIL A
MEASUREMENTS IN MM

STRING

SCREW M 12×180

STEP

SECTION E—E

INSERT SCREW HERE,
THEN PUSH RIGHT

FOOT PRESSURE POINTS

AFTER BUILDING
IN STAIRCASE,
WELD HERE

FFL
FDS

TO BE CEMENTED TO
FLOOR IN SITU

6.3.3 Helical stairs with cut strings

The strings in this cable-suspended stair, which act as beams running through the structure, appear to be static. The suspension cables are fitted with distancers at the points where they cross the balustrade handrail, which gives the balustrade extra rigidity. The type of wood used here is mat-sealed Afzelia. The preliminary sketch (below) of the staircase perspective is a way of developing perception and creates the conditions from which correct construction and a well-thought-out design can evolve.

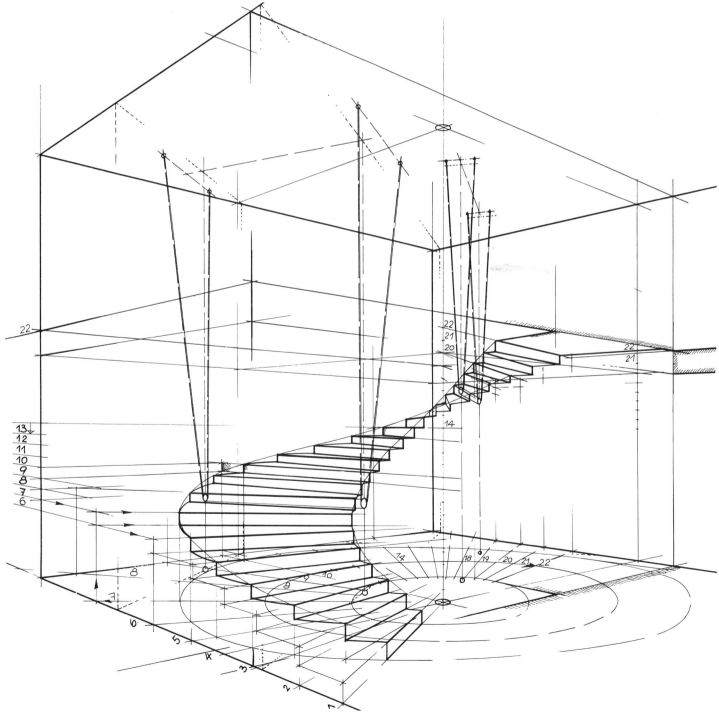

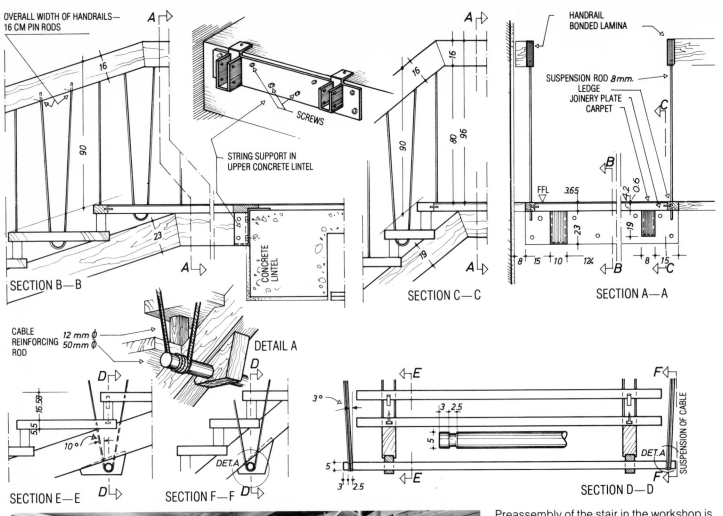

SECTION B—B

OVERALL WIDTH OF HANDRAILS— 16 CM PIN RODS

16

90

23

SCREWS

STRING SUPPORT IN UPPER CONCRETE LINTEL

CONCRETE LINTEL

SECTION C—C

16

16

90

60

96

19

SECTION A—A

HANDRAIL BONDED LAMINA

SUSPENSION ROD *8mm.*
LEDGE
JOINERY PLATE
CARPET

FFL 3.65

4.2 0.6

23

19

8 15 10 12.4 8 15

CABLE REINFORCING ROD

12 mm φ
50mm φ

DETAIL A

SECTION E—E

16.59

5.5

10°

SECTION F—F

DET.A

3°

3 2.5

5

5

3 2.5

E

E

F

F

DET.A

SUSPENSION OF CABLE

SECTION D—D

Preassembly of the stair in the workshop is illustrated at left.

Note the way in which the treads have been mounted in this stair: they are suspended at the front edge on cylindrical rods. A particularly thoughtful solution has been found here for the construction of the bottom step, newel posts, and segments, and for fixing the handrails.

The connection of strings and treads in this stair is highly individual. Fixing by bolt and socket gives a high degree of stability; in addition, wooden dowels are sunk and movement of treads is avoided by hammering in nails at an angle. The steps are finished with a special brass edge strip.

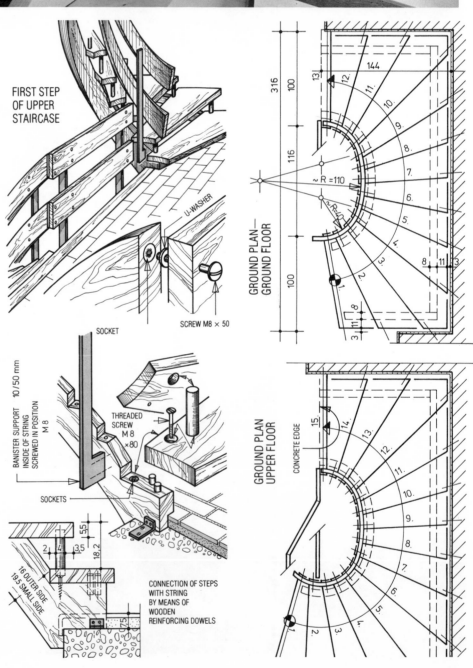

FIRST STEP OF UPPER STAIRCASE

U-WASHER

SCREW M8 × 50

GROUND PLAN— GROUND FLOOR

316
100
13
144
12.
11.
10.
9.
116
8.
~ R =110
7.
6.
5.
4.
3.
100
2.
1.
8 11 3
3 11 8

SOCKET

BANISTER SUPPORT 10/50 mm INSIDE OF STRING SCREWED IN POSITION M 8

THREADED SCREW M 8 ×80

SOCKETS

55
2 4 3,5
18,2
16 OUTER SIDE
19,5 SMALL SIDE
75

CONNECTION OF STEPS WITH STRING BY MEANS OF WOODEN REINFORCING DOWELS

GROUND PLAN UPPER FLOOR

CONCRETE EDGE

15.
14.
13.
12.
11.
10.
9.
8.
7.
6.
5.
4.
3.
2.
1.

The staircase shown in these three photographs has a supported spine string. It is particularly worth noting the way in which the line of force runs along the central string, which is not fixed. The wide part of the fifth tread is post-tensioned. The fence-style handrails create an interesting effect.

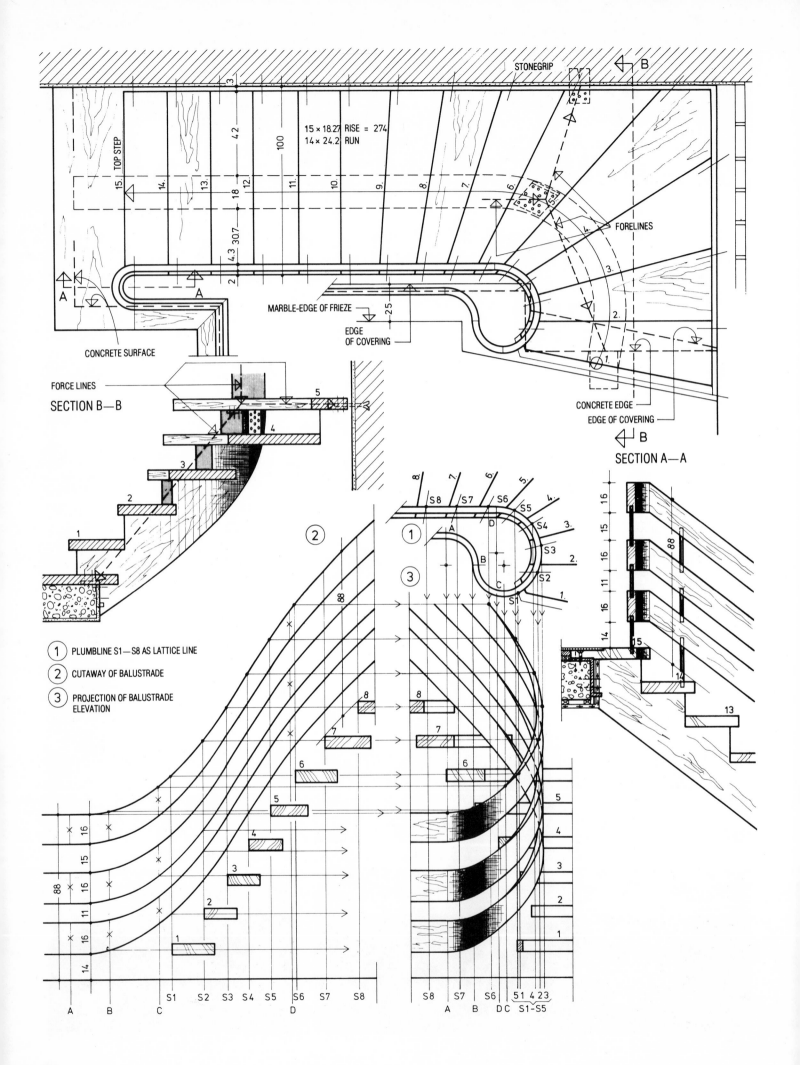

STONEGRIP

15×18.27 RISE = 274
14×24.2 RUN

TOP STEP

15   14.   13.   12.   11.   10.   9.   8.   7.   6.

42   100   18   4.3 307   2   25

FORELINES

MARBLE-EDGE OF FRIEZE

EDGE
OF COVERING

CONCRETE SURFACE

CONCRETE EDGE

EDGE OF COVERING

B

SECTION A—A

FORCE LINES

SECTION B—B

① PLUMBLINE S1—S8 AS LATTICE LINE

② CUTAWAY OF BALUSTRADE

③ PROJECTION OF BALUSTRADE
ELEVATION

S8   S7   S6   S5   S4   S3   S2   S1

88

16   15   16   11   16   14

S1   S2   S3   S4   S5   S6   S7   S8

A   B   C   D

S8   S7   S6   51 4 23

A   B   D C   S1—S5

74

Here, the curved fixed-spine string acts as a support for the entire staircase. The balustrade panels are made from 5-mm-thick sheet steel; a cutting torch has been used to shape this unusual pattern and the surface of the panels has then been sprayed mat white. The dark shade of the treads and handrails and the light string and white panels contrast pleasingly with the pale green walls.

By boarding in the area beneath the half-landing, the creation of a dust-trap has been avoided. An impression of the total width of the stairwell is retained by a "see-through" stair construction for the flight of stairs leading to the first floor. The material used here is light oak.

The stair below has been
installed in a relatively small
surface area and is completely
in keeping with the interior
design of the hallway. The
concept is simple,
straightforward, and lacking in
embellishment, thus allowing
the finely sculptured lines of the
lower part of the handrail to
stand out to full effect. The
wood used is mat-sealed
darkened oak.

Here, a concrete flower box shields the stairway from the entrance door of the house; a convection heater has been installed, beneath the flower box to provide a warm-air barrier against cold entering the house by way of the front door. The height of the flower box is determined by the height of the top corner of the wall string.

The supporting wall (1) is constructed from plywood-type laminated segments that have been loose-tongue jointed (2). The notched riser (3) and the tread, which has a fitted edge strip (4), are glued rigid to the supporting wall when the staircase is assembled; this is done with the aid of holding blocks (5) bolted and glued in position.

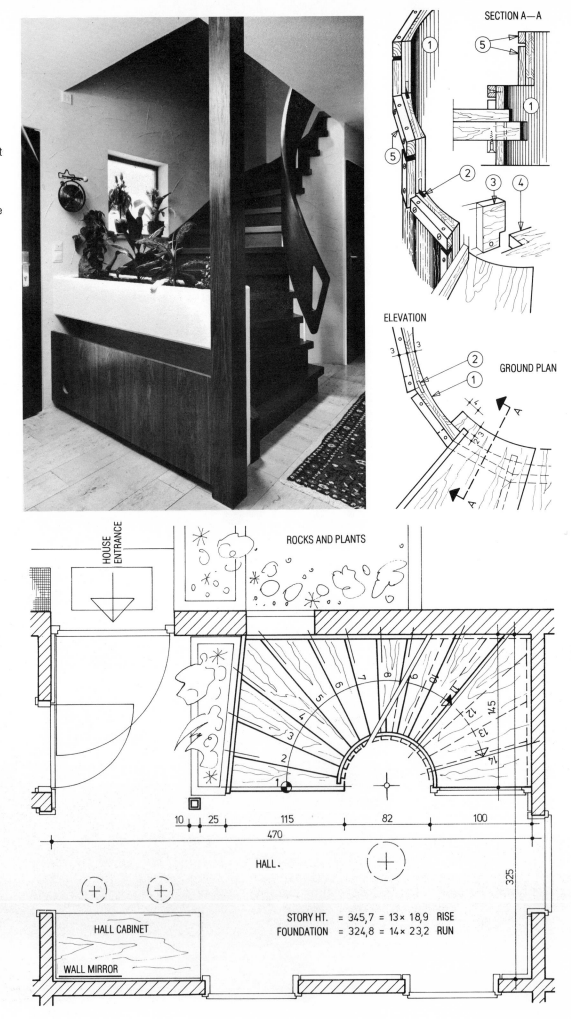

SECTION A—A

ELEVATION

GROUND PLAN

HOUSE ENTRANCE

ROCKS AND PLANTS

HALL.

HALL CABINET

WALL MIRROR

STORY HT. = 345,7 = 13 × 18,9 RISE
FOUNDATION = 324,8 = 14 × 23,2 RUN

10   25   115   82   100

470

325

In this relatively small stairwell, the second step has been developed to serve as a landing slab, thus allowing the stair to rise steeply from the lower floor. Both treads and risers are tapered. The 15-mm-thick steel rods have been drilled in deeply to ensure maximum stability and the three-cornered upright at the bottom step holds the balustrade absolutely firm. The wood is darkened oak.

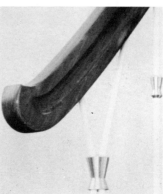

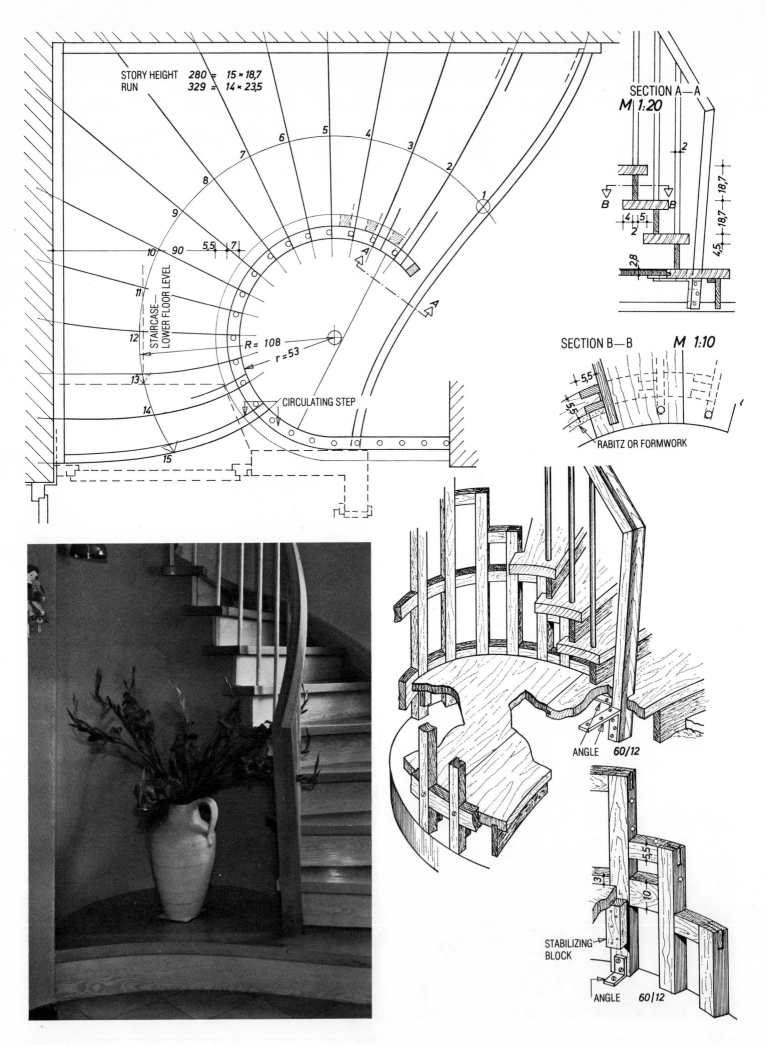

STORY HEIGHT 280 = 15 × 18,7
RUN 329 = 14 × 23,5

SECTION A—A
M 1:20

SECTION B—B   M 1:10

RABITZ OR FORMWORK

STAIRCASE—
LOWER FLOOR LEVEL

R = 108
r = 53

CIRCULATING STEP

ANGLE 60/12

STABILIZING
BLOCK

ANGLE 60/12

The quarterhelical staircase illustrated below has a wall string, but a somewhat different form of support on the outer side. Instead of the more normal construction with an outer string, a framework construction has been used, which serves simultaneously as a plaster base on the outer side. Its inner side has a chipboard cladding which is positioned after assembly of the staircase and provides a smooth finish for the superstructure. As shown in the diagram on the following page, a perfect finish can be achieved by bolting the treads and risers to the framework. The baluster boards are sunk into the treads to a depth of 8 cm and plugged, so that the balustrade is rendered secure and rigid in both directions. The treads and handrails are darkened oak, while risers and baluster boards are pine; the owner has also used pine cladding on the stairwell ceiling.

SECTION A—A

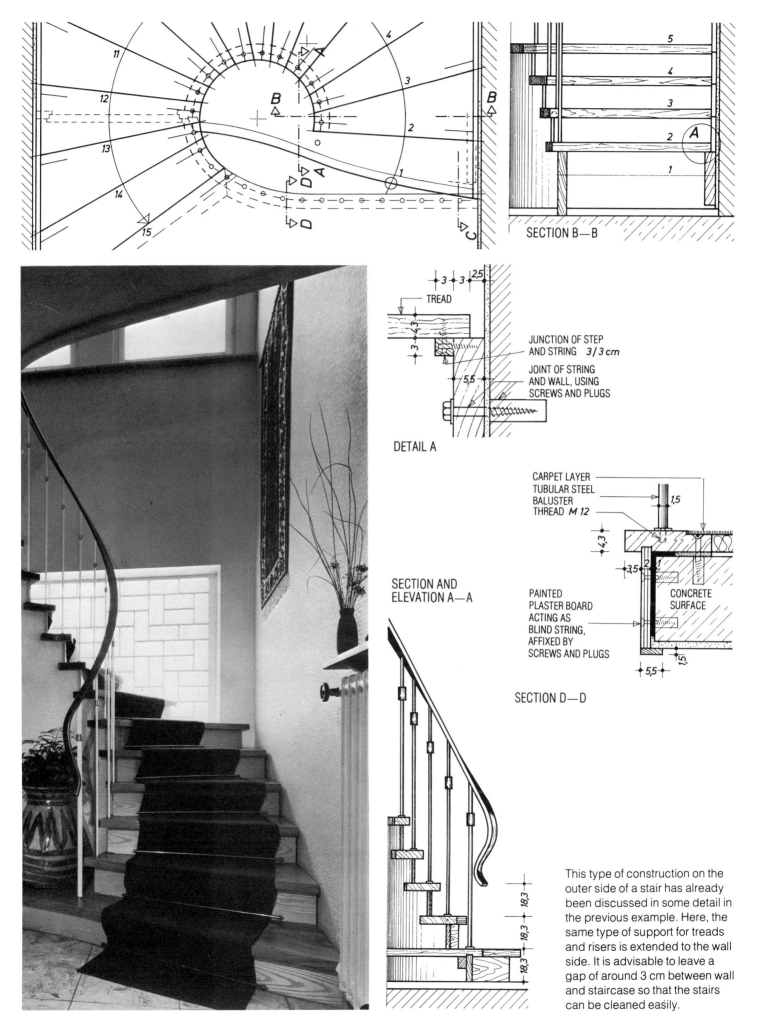

SECTION B—B

---

3 · 3 · 2,5

↓ TREAD

3 · 4,3

5,5

JUNCTION OF STEP
AND STRING 3/3 cm

JOINT OF STRING
AND WALL, USING
SCREWS AND PLUGS

DETAIL A

CARPET LAYER
TUBULAR STEEL
BALUSTER
THREAD M 12

1,5

4,3

3,5 2 1

PAINTED
PLASTER BOARD
ACTING AS
BLIND STRING,
AFFIXED BY
SCREWS AND PLUGS

CONCRETE
SURFACE

1,5

5,5

SECTION D—D

SECTION AND
ELEVATION A—A

18,3

18,3 18,3

18,3

This type of construction on the
outer side of a stair has already
been discussed in some detail in
the previous example. Here, the
same type of support for treads
and risers is extended to the wall
side. It is advisable to leave a
gap of around 3 cm between wall
and staircase so that the stairs
can be cleaned easily.

83

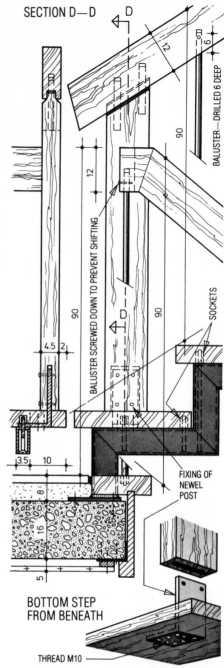

SECTION D—D

BALUSTER—DRILLED 6 DEEP

BALUSTER SCREWED DOWN TO PREVENT SHIFTING

SOCKETS

FIXING OF NEWEL POST

BOTTOM STEP FROM BENEATH

THREAD M10

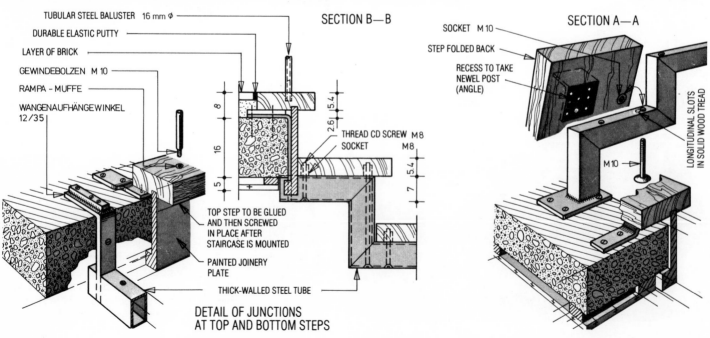

TUBULAR STEEL BALUSTER 16 mm ⌀

DURABLE ELASTIC PUTTY

LAYER OF BRICK

GEWINDEBOLZEN M 10

RAMPA - MUFFE

WANGENAUFHÄNGEWINKEL
12 / 35

SECTION B—B

THREAD CD SCREW M 8

SOCKET M 8

TOP STEP TO BE GLUED
AND THEN SCREWED
IN PLACE AFTER
STAIRCASE IS MOUNTED

PAINTED JOINERY
PLATE

THICK-WALLED STEEL TUBE

**DETAIL OF JUNCTIONS
AT TOP AND BOTTOM STEPS**

SECTION A—A

SOCKET M 10

STEP FOLDED BACK

RECESS TO TAKE
NEWEL POST
(ANGLE)

M 10

LONGITUDINAL SLOTS
IN SOLID WOOD TREAD

This is a half-helical stair with an infrastructure of steel tubes. These tubes, measuring 35 x 70 x 5 mm, mitred and welded, form the basic construction here and act as a substitute for strings. The junctions with the concrete ceiling are important. The treads are connected to the steel tubes by means of M10 countersunk screws and, in order to achieve the best possible junction, tube sockets are sunk into the treads. Steel rods are used as balusters. By means of drilling in these 16-mm rods to a depth of 5 to 6 cm, the balustrade achieves the proscribed level of stability, since they act as fixed supports. In addition, the newel posts are protected against lateral shearing by heavy bearing angles.

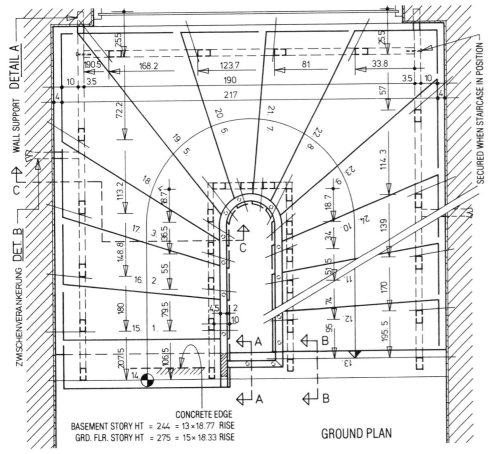

CONCRETE EDGE
BASEMENT STORY HT = 244 = 13 × 18.77 RISE
GRD. FLR. STORY HT = 275 = 15 × 18.33 RISE

GROUND PLAN

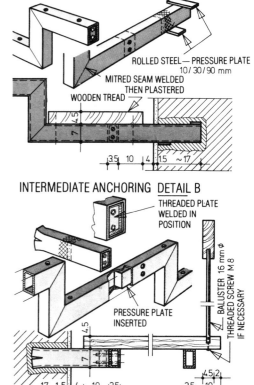

WALL SUPPORT DETAIL A

ROLLED STEEL — PRESSURE PLATE
10 / 30 / 90 mm
MITRED SEAM WELDED THEN PLASTERED
WOODEN TREAD

INTERMEDIATE ANCHORING DETAIL B

THREADED PLATE WELDED IN POSITION

PRESSURE PLATE INSERTED

BALUSTER 16 mm ⌀
THREADED SCREW M 8 IF NECESSARY

SECTION C—C

The illustration on the left shows a staircase with the same basic construction. The flight leading to the basement is reinforced concrete with cast-stone steps, hence the lack of a handrail wreath portion at the turn of the stairs.

This example is proof of the fact that a staircase can be comfortable and stylish even when little space is available. The treads are connected to each other by special bearer angles, which transmit support from the steel stays in the parapet to the lower section of the upper stair.

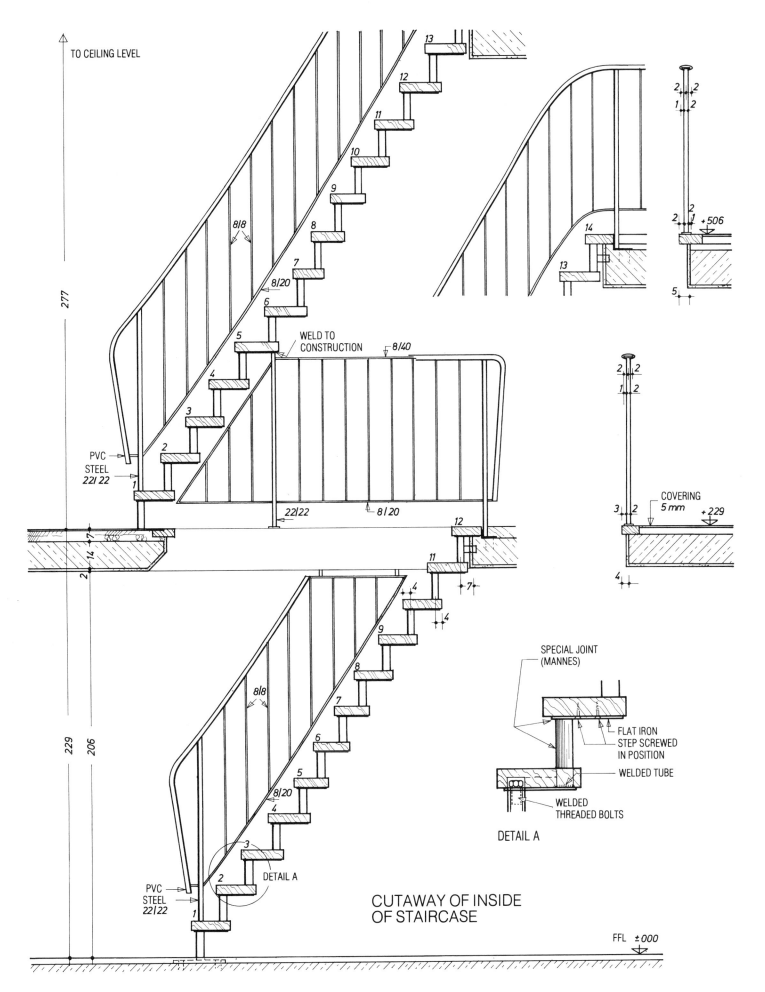

TO CEILING LEVEL

277

229

206

PVC
STEEL
22/22

1

2

3

4

5

6

7

8/20

8

8/8

9

10

11

12

13

WELD TO
CONSTRUCTION

8/40

22/22

8/20

12

11

4

7

4

9

8

7

8/8

6

5

8/20

4

3

DETAIL A

2

PVC
STEEL
22/22

1

CUTAWAY OF INSIDE
OF STAIRCASE

FFL ±000

2 2
1 2

2   2
1   +506

5

14

13

2 2
1 2

3 2

COVERING
5 mm

4

+ 229

SPECIAL JOINT
(MANNES)

FLAT IRON
STEP SCREWED
IN POSITION

WELDED TUBE

WELDED
THREADED BOLTS

DETAIL A

The balustrade in this marble stair is mahogany, stained blackish brown and given a dull mat seal. The material used for the supports is solid japanned brass.

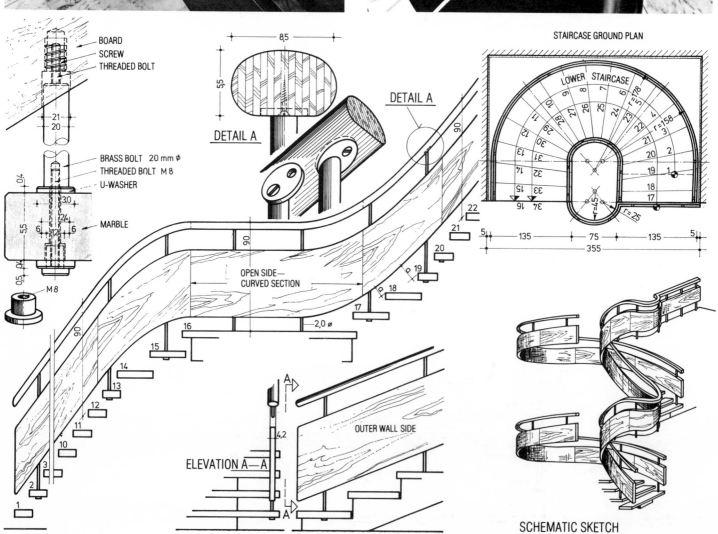

BOARD
SCREW
THREADED BOLT

21
20

BRASS BOLT 20 mm ∅
THREADED BOLT M 8
U-WASHER

0,4
30
5,5   24
6   6
12
0,4
0,5   M 8

MARBLE

M 8

DETAIL A

8,5
5,5

DETAIL A

90

90

22
21
20
19
18
17

2,0 ∅

16
15
14
13
12
11
10
3
2
1

OPEN SIDE—
CURVED SECTION

90

A
4,2

ELEVATION A—A

A

OUTER WALL SIDE

STAIRCASE GROUND PLAN

LOWER STAIRCASE
8   7
9
10   r=178
26 25 24
27   23   4
28   29   22   r=158
30   21   3
31   20   2
32   19   1
33   18
34 15   17
16   r=45   r=25

5   135   75   135   5
355

SCHEMATIC SKETCH

88

A number of materials have been employed in the design of this reception area at a concrete works. The sweep of the stair and the recessing of the ceiling relieve the horizontal and vertical texture of the room.

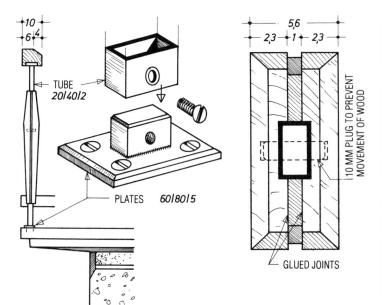

TUBE 20/40/2

PLATES 60/80/5

5,6
2,3 · 1 · 2,3

10 MM PLUG TO PREVENT MOVEMENT OF WOOD

GLUED JOINTS

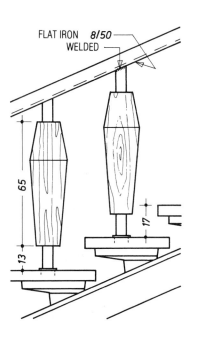

FLAT IRON 8/50
WELDED

65

13

17

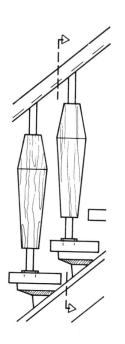

The molded light metal wall panels, which are set into the raw surface of the wall, blend perfectly with the mat-finished balusters. Ten-mm Plexiglas fills the space between the handrails and marble steps and acts as a guardrail.

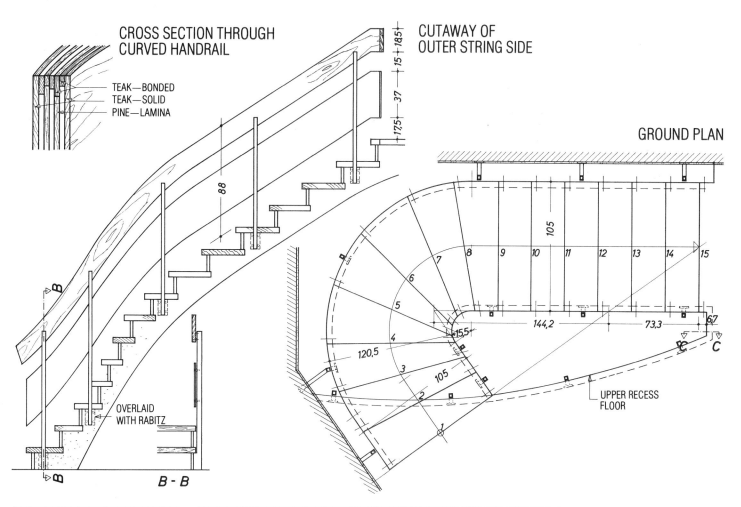

CROSS SECTION THROUGH CURVED HANDRAIL

TEAK—BONDED
TEAK—SOLID
PINE—LAMINA

CUTAWAY OF OUTER STRING SIDE

185
15
37
175
88

GROUND PLAN

105
7 8 9 10 11 12 13 14 15
+15,5
120,5
105
144,2 73,3 67
C C
UPPER RECESS FLOOR

B
OVERLAID WITH RABITZ
B
B - B

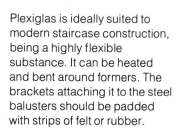

Plexiglas is ideally suited to modern staircase construction, being a highly flexible substance. It can be heated and bent around formers. The brackets attaching it to the steel balusters should be padded with strips of felt or rubber.

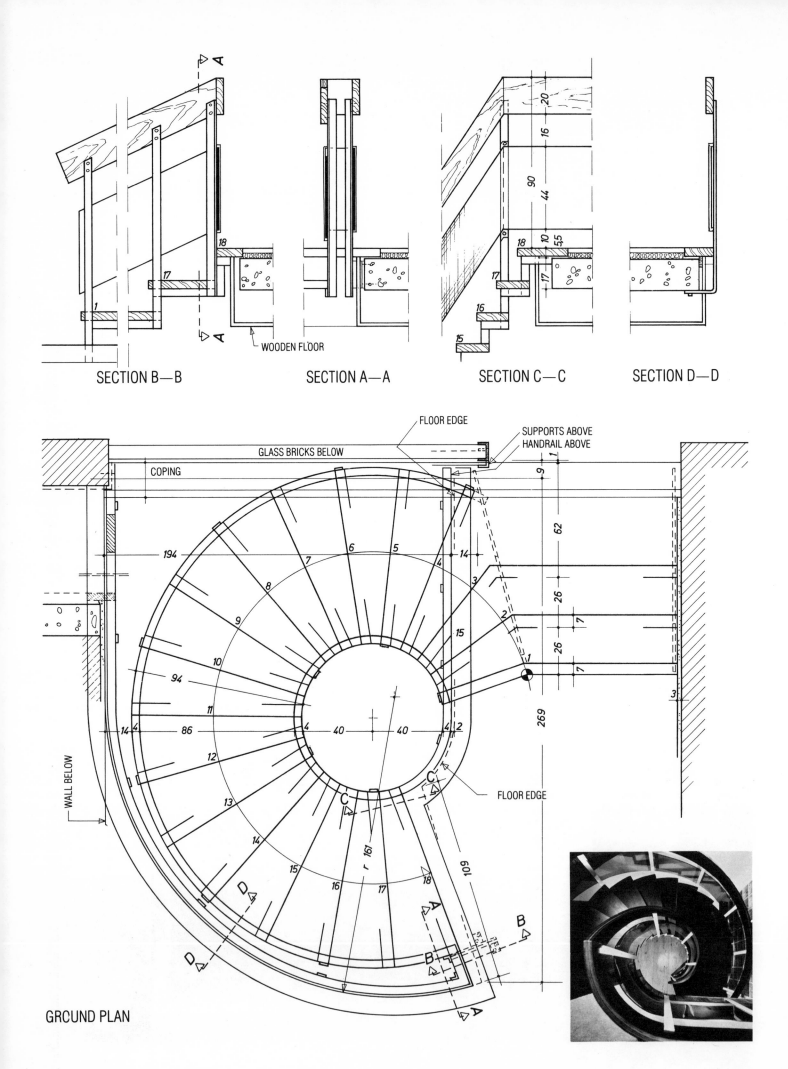

SECTION B—B

SECTION A—A

SECTION C—C

SECTION D—D

18

17

1

20

16

90

44

18

10

55

17

16

15

WOODEN FLOOR

FLOOR EDGE

SUPPORTS ABOVE
HANDRAIL ABOVE

GLASS BRICKS BELOW

COPING

194

6   5

7

8   4   14

9   3

10   15   2

94   1

86   4   12

11   4

12   40   40

13   C

14   C

15   161

16   17   18

269   109

1

9

62

26

7

26

7

3

FLOOR EDGE

WALL BELOW

D   D   A   B   B   A

GROUND PLAN

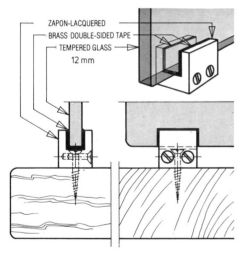

ZAPON-LACQUERED
BRASS DOUBLE-SIDED TAPE
TEMPERED GLASS
12 mm

The tempered-glass panels affixed to this oak staircase by brass clips blend in well with this somewhat austere reception area in a bank.

The sketches below show three ways of using tempered glass or Plexiglas in this type of structure.

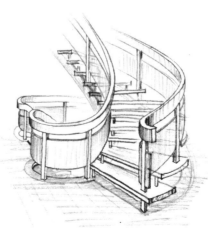

The treads here measure 6 x 50 cm and are bolted between the steel balusters. In the lower tread section, sockets are sunk into the facings of the treads and the treads should therefore be laminated. The material used for handrails and strings is pine, while the treads are darkened oak. The staircase has a clean, functional effect against the background of limestone walls and concrete honeycomb windows.

As in the staircase previously described, two sections of equal width have been achieved here. The mahogany treads, strings, and handrails, together with the white-painted balusters and the finely plastered wall surfaces give this stairwell an almost festive appearance.

The illustration on the right shows the basement balustrade; the lower part of the parapet on the ground floor is also visible.

The renovation of a menswear store made redesigning both these staircases desirable. The 70-mm laminated timber treads are carpeted and cantilever from a free concrete spine string. The front edges of the treads are protected by brass edge strips.

The blind strings bolted to this concrete stair and the curved handrail are veneered marsh oak; both treads and risers are carpeted and, here too, brass edge strips have been used for protection against mechanical damage.

This stair leads from the main living area to a secondary lower floor. The strings are welded 10 x 70 mm rolled steel, and the wall string is fixed at a distance of 1.2 m by means of brackets cemented to the wall. An effect of cantilevering has been achieved by welding the upper part of the treads to the sheet steel brackets; this method of fixing has also been used at the foot of the stair and this has significant static advantages as far as the outer string is concerned. This construction is exceptionally stable and is light and elegant in appearance.

TOP STEP

FIXING SECTIONS OF PARAPET

SECTION C—C

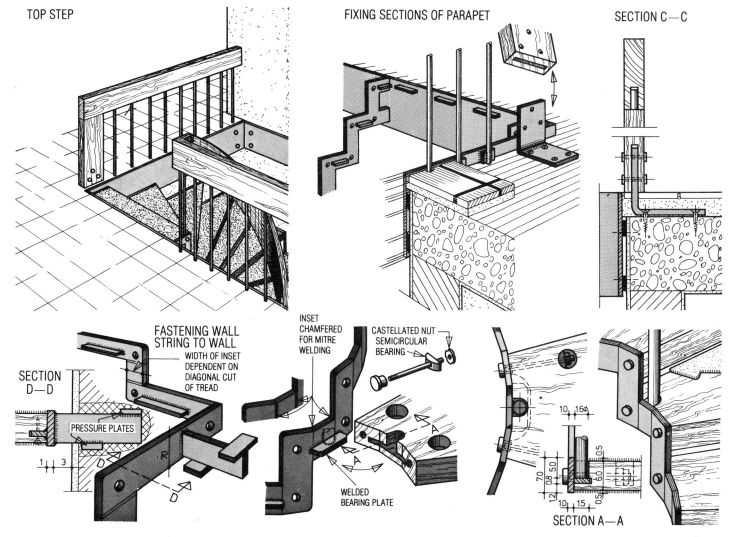

SECTION D—D

FASTENING WALL STRING TO WALL

WIDTH OF INSET DEPENDENT ON DIAGONAL CUT OF TREAD

PRESSURE PLATES

INSET CHAMFERED FOR MITRE WELDING

CASTELLATED NUT SEMICIRCULAR BEARING

WELDED BEARING PLATE

SECTION A—A

In this semicircular stair, the risers are fixed to the reinforced concrete wall by means of gravity plugs, thus acting as cantilevers. In order to minimize the noise level, strips of felt are placed between the upper edge of the riser and its junction with the tread, as the diagram shows. The connection between the back edge of the treads and the risers is reinforced by welding in bearing blocks, so that loading from above does not come to bear on the countersunk screws. A hardwood nosing is fixed by a loose-tongue joint and glued. The edge strips, which are adhered to the facings of the treads, are 3-mm curved veneer. The handrail, 4.8 × 13 cm thick and made up of 3-mm bonded laminae, is rendered much easier to manufacture by the introduction of a straight parapet linking the curved sections. The vertical working members, which are of painted tubular steel, are drilled deep into the handrail to give extra rigidity to the structure, making it unnecessary to include newel posts or stabilizers here.

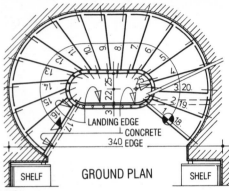

GROUND PLAN

LANDING EDGE
CONCRETE
340 EDGE
SHELF
SHELF

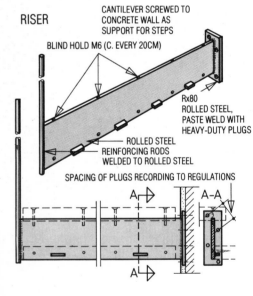

RISER

CANTILEVER SCREWED TO CONCRETE WALL AS SUPPORT FOR STEPS

BLIND HOLD M6 (C. EVERY 20CM)

Rx80 ROLLED STEEL, PASTE WELD WITH HEAVY-DUTY PLUGS

ROLLED STEEL REINFORCING RODS WELDED TO ROLLED STEEL

SPACING OF PLUGS RECORDING TO REGULATIONS

A–A

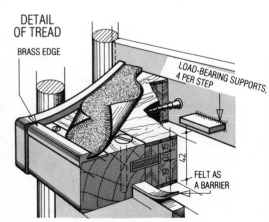

DETAIL OF TREAD

BRASS EDGE

LOAD-BEARING SUPPORTS, 4 PER STEP

FELT AS A BARRIER

Extra storage space is created by drawing back the partition at the bottom section of the stair. All visible steel and wooden elements have been colorfully painted, while the treads themselves are lined with carpet.

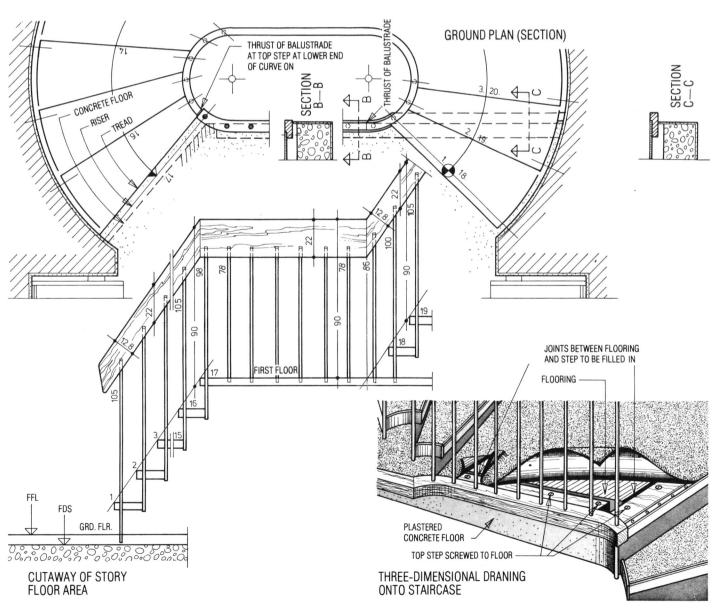

GROUND PLAN (SECTION)

THRUST OF BALUSTRADE AT TOP STEP AT LOWER END OF CURVE ON

SECTION B—B

THRUST OF BALUSTRADE

SECTION C—C

CONCRETE FLOOR
RISER
TREAD

FIRST FLOOR

FFL
FDS
GRD. FLR.

CUTAWAY OF STORY
FLOOR AREA

JOINTS BETWEEN FLOORING
AND STEP TO BE FILLED IN

FLOORING

PLASTERED
CONCRETE FLOOR

TOP STEP SCREWED TO FLOOR

THREE-DIMENSIONAL DRANING
ONTO STAIRCASE

99

6.4 Stylized stairs—straight-flight and curved

In order to display this semicircular wooden staircase to best effect, its wrought-iron balustrade is continued beneath the outer string to connect with the blockstep, which has been widened and extended. An interesting feature, which is clearly visible in this photograph, is the blind string that continues as far as the penultimate step. The strings and handrails are oak, bonded in layers; the 60-mm treads are laminated and carpeted in moss green. Balusters are 25 × 25 mm rectangular steel and the decorative panels are 5 × 20 mm grey-green patina-coated rolled steel.

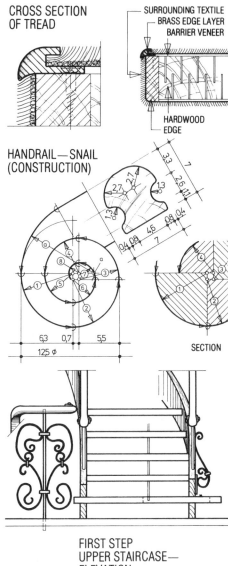

CROSS SECTION
OF TREAD

SURROUNDING TEXTILE
BRASS EDGE LAYER
BARRIER VENEER

HARDWOOD
EDGE

HANDRAIL—SNAIL
(CONSTRUCTION)

SECTION

125 ϕ

FIRST STEP
UPPER STAIRCASE—
ELEVATION

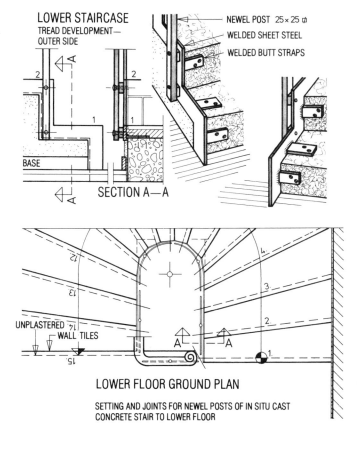

LOWER STAIRCASE
TREAD DEVELOPMENT—
OUTER SIDE

NEWEL POST 25 × 25 ϕ
WELDED SHEET STEEL
WELDED BUTT STRAPS

BASE

SECTION A—A

LOWER FLOOR GROUND PLAN

UNPLASTERED
WALL TILES

SETTING AND JOINTS FOR NEWEL POSTS OF IN SITU CAST
CONCRETE STAIR TO LOWER FLOOR

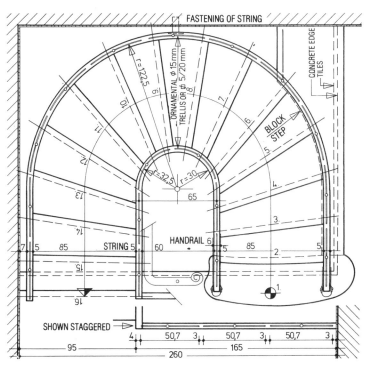

FASTENING OF STRING

CONCRETE EDGE
TILES

r = 122.5
ORNAMENTAL ϕ 15 mm
TRELLIS OR ϕ 5/20 mm

BLOCK
STEP

r = 32.5   r = 30

65

HANDRAIL

STRING

SHOWN STAGGERED

95
260

50,7   3   50,7   3   50,7   3
165

UPPER FLOOR GROUND PLAN

101

An eye-catching decorative wrought-iron panel standing in front of
the stair takes the place of both balustrade and landing parapet and
creates a particularly charming effect. The strings are lime-washed
and stained grey.

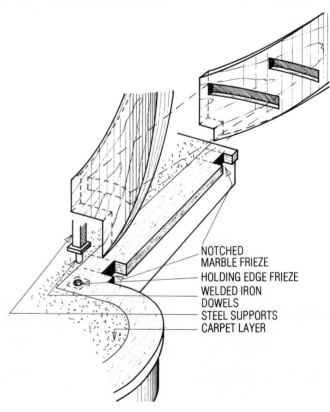

NOTCHED
MARBLE FRIEZE
HOLDING EDGE FRIEZE
WELDED IRON
DOWELS
STEEL SUPPORTS
CARPET LAYER

The height of this Great Hall is modified by the effect of the flight of stairs leading to a gangway at half-height. The blind string is bolted to the concrete steps before the marble treads are installed. Effective use has been made of flat balusters to break up an otherwise monotonous line of delicately turned rods. Oak, stained grey-green and given a mat silk seal, is used.

This semicircular open-riser stair was installed in a converted building; it was required to blend with the original pillars and beams, which had been restored and kept. The outer string, which is approximately 10 m long, is suspended from above on 20-mm steel suspension rods. The bottom step of the upper stair is flush with the floor and set back so that horizontal and sloping balustrades can finish at the same level. The wood used is fumed oak.

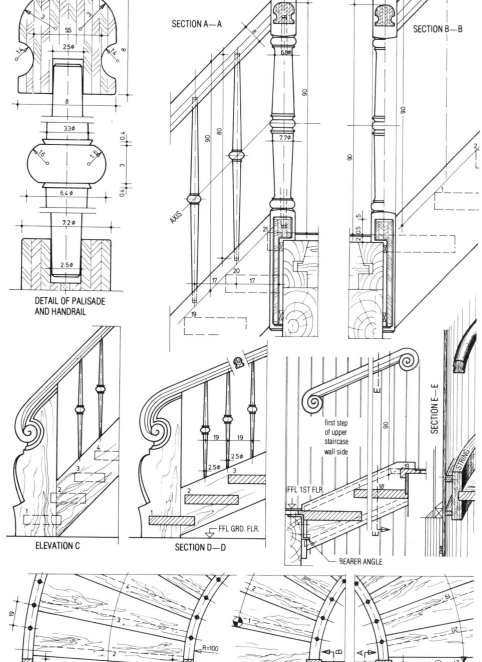

DETAIL OF PALISADE AND HANDRAIL

SECTION A—A

SECTION B—B

ELEVATION C

SECTION D—D

first step of upper staircase wall side

FFL 1ST FLR.

FFL GRD. FLR.

SECTION E—E

STRING

BEARER ANGLE

The treads are arranged in such a way that the handrails can be set at the same height.

GROUND PLAN OF FIRST STEP

ELEVATION C

FIRST STEP OF UPPER STAIRCASE

FIRST STEP OF LOWER STAIRCASE

BEAMS

R=100

The great amount of light entering the stairwell makes the use of dark, fumed oak feasible. Safety is assured by the fact that light falls on the front edges of the treads.

This stair had to harmonize with heavy baroque furniture. Although its execution is on much simplified lines, without the rich wood-carving associated with baroque style, various characteristics of that era are noticeable in its design. Note in particular the finish of the balusters where they meet strings and handrail. The design of the newels is developed from the form of the balusters.

These ceiling coffers, which are Chinese in origin, are strongly colored and are echoed in the wall coverings, which are of a paler shade. The plain (mahogany) tone of the stair is restrained in comparison, but an impact is nevertheless created by the form of the staircase with its powerful strings and handrails. The landing slab can serve to display vases or ornaments.

Alternative proposal

Staircase ground plan

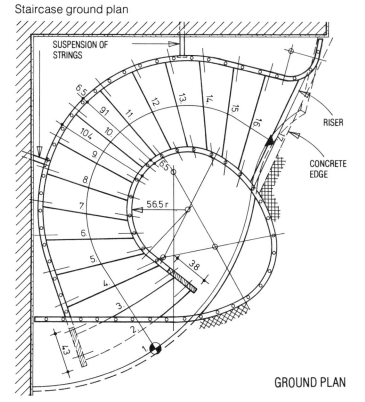

SUSPENSION OF
STRINGS

RISER

CONCRETE
EDGE

56.5 r

38

43

GROUND PLAN

This illustration shows the stair photographed from ground level up.

The illustration below shows the same stair, this time photographed from the top.

This stair and the blind ceiling beams are oak, stained coffee-brown; they form an integrated unit with the Mansonia-parquet floor and the arches of the doors.

In order to avoid any possibility of warping in these treads, they have been manufactured from 42-mm blockboard which has been adhered to 6-mm sawn veneer. The risers, constructed in the same way, although only 20-mm thick, are screwed and bonded to the treads. This avoids creaking in use. An interesting feature is the joint lines of the ceiling veneers.

Below right is an example of how
impressive the use of a wreath portion can
be in a stair with correct dimensions.
Equal mortise widths in the landings and
treads, measured to the center of the
string depth, produce a rectilinear profile.

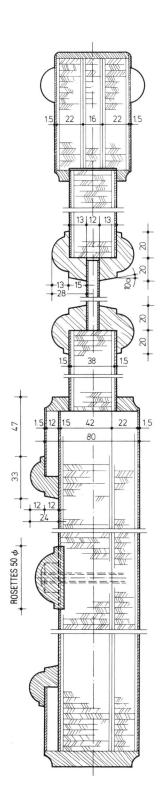

In this elegant stylized stair, the balustrade has a powerful effect, which is enhanced by the way in which the treads are fixed by visible screws. The curved decorative beadings and infill panels are 3-mm counter veneers.

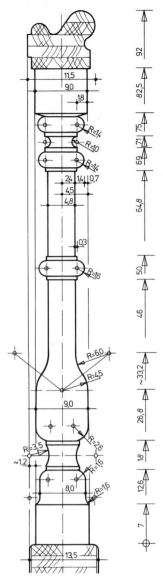

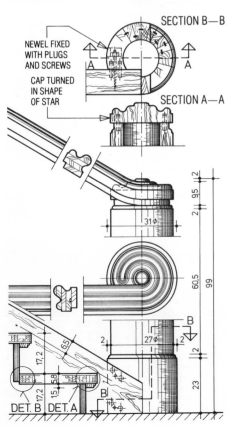

SECTION B—B

NEWEL FIXED
WITH PLUGS
AND SCREWS

CAP TURNED
IN SHAPE
OF STAR

SECTION A—A

DET. B   DET. A

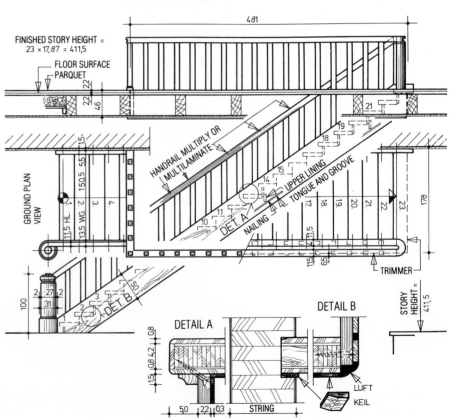

FINISHED STORY HEIGHT =
23 × 17,87 = 411,5

FLOOR SURFACE
PARQUET

GROUND PLAN
VIEW

HANDRAIL MULTIPLY OR
MULTILAMINATE

UPPER LINING
TONGUE AND GROOVE

NAILING

DET. A

DET. B

TRIMMER

STORY
HEIGHT =
411,5

DETAIL A

DETAIL B

STRING

LUFT

KEIL

114

For static reasons and because of fire regulations, the strings here are laminated oak, with a 3-mm surface veneer. The treads and blockboard have an 8-mm oak surround; risers are 20-mm plywood oak veneered at the facings (1.5 mm). The newel post has a hollow core and is made up of loose-tongue jointed and bonded sections (to prevent cracking). Treads and risers are mortised approximately 3 mm wider to allow for easier assembly of this somewhat heavy staircase. Before the risers are screwed (nailed) in position, the treads must be wedged with hardwood driven up and forward. The wedges should be glued in or pinned so that they do not become loose in the event of slight warping. This wedging procedure ensures that both treads and risers sit absolutely firm.

This stair is the perfect complement to the valuable furnishings and *objets d'art* in the room. Strings, treads, and risers are oak-veneered laminboard. The material used in the handrails is solid oak, bonded in layers.

CROSS SECTION OF BALUSTRADE— SHAPE OF BALUSTERS

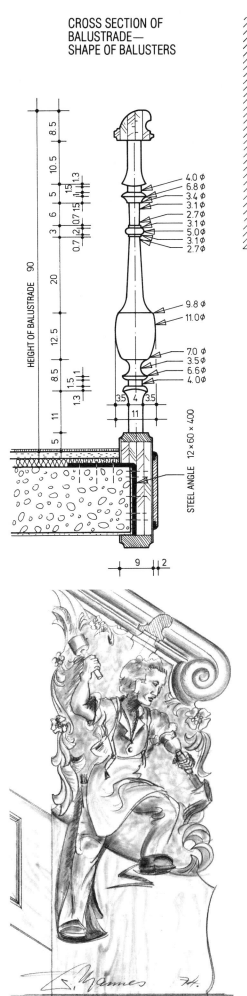

HEIGHT OF BALUSTRADE 90

8.5
10.5
1.3
15
15
5
6
2.07
0.7
2
3
4.0 Φ
6.8 Φ
3.4 Φ
3.1 Φ
2.7 Φ
3.1 Φ
5.0 Φ
3.1 Φ
2.7 Φ

20

9.8 Φ
11.0 Φ

12.5

70 Φ
3.5 Φ
6.6 Φ
4.0 Φ

8.5
1.5
1.1
1.3

35 4 3.5

11

11

5

STEEL ANGLE 12 × 60 × 400

9   2

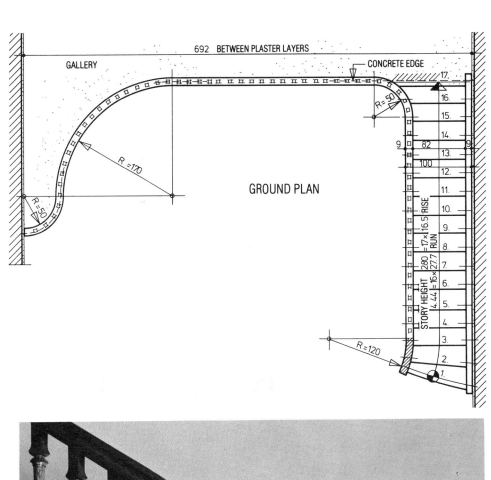

692   BETWEEN PLASTER LAYERS

GALLERY

CONCRETE EDGE

GROUND PLAN

R =170

R =50

R =50

R =120

R= 50

17.
16.
15.
14.
13.
12.
11.
10.
9.
8.
7.
6.
5.
4.
3.
2.
1.

82
100
9   9

STORY HEIGHT 4.44 = 16×27.7 RUN
280 = 17×16.5 RISE

117

In this historic house, which is under a preservation order, a wooden balustrade has been added to a marble-covered reinforced concrete stair. Several sections of the original balustrade were found and could be used. Heavy-duty rolled steel bearer angles at intervals of approximately 80 cm support the reinforced concrete skeleton of the stair at the outer edge. The base of the balustrade is supported from beneath by 8 × 50 mm wood screws. The baluster boards, which are glued in position, and which are inclined to some extent at the wreaths, make this balustrade exceptionally firm.

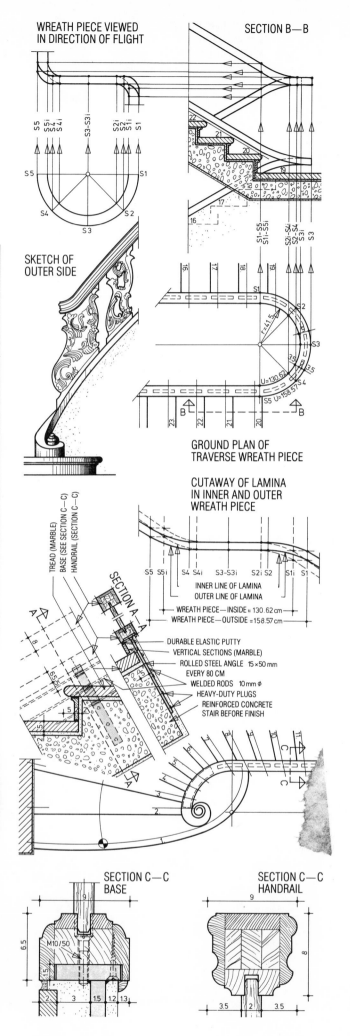

WREATH PIECE VIEWED IN DIRECTION OF FLIGHT

SECTION B—B

SKETCH OF OUTER SIDE

GROUND PLAN OF TRAVERSE WREATH PIECE

CUTAWAY OF LAMINA IN INNER AND OUTER WREATH PIECE

INNER LINE OF LAMINA
OUTER LINE OF LAMINA
WREATH PIECE—INSIDE = 130.62 cm
WREATH PIECE—OUTSIDE = 158.57 cm

DURABLE ELASTIC PUTTY
VERTICAL SECTIONS (MARBLE)
ROLLED STEEL ANGLE 15 × 50 mm EVERY 80 CM
WELDED RODS 10 mm ⌀
HEAVY-DUTY PLUGS
REINFORCED CONCRETE STAIR BEFORE FINISH

TREAD (MARBLE)
BASE (SEE SECTION C—C)
HANDRAIL (SECTION C—C)

SECTION A—A

SECTION C—C BASE

SECTION C—C HANDRAIL

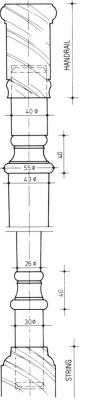

The colors red, white, and beige lend this stairwell a festive touch; the handrails are white mahogany, while the treads are carpeted in red. An interesting effect is created by the filigree-like balustrade in this small, steep stair.

The principal sections of this stair are laminated, though the treads are provided with hardwood edges. Solid oak is used for the newels and balusters. The newel post has a hollow core; this allows the wood to move slightly, without cracks forming, following installation.

6.5 Spiral (helical) staircases

The central column of this spiral staircase with winders is constructed in sections, then bolted together with a 24-mm-thick screw. If the treads shear slightly following installation, the cap at the top of the column can be removed and the screw tightened to counteract this effect. The treads are 42-mm-thick blockboards, to which 8-mm-thick laminae have been affixed both above and below. The materials used in this stair are darkened oak and smoke-grey tinted Plexiglas, bent around formers when heated; the central newel and balusters have been painted mat-white.

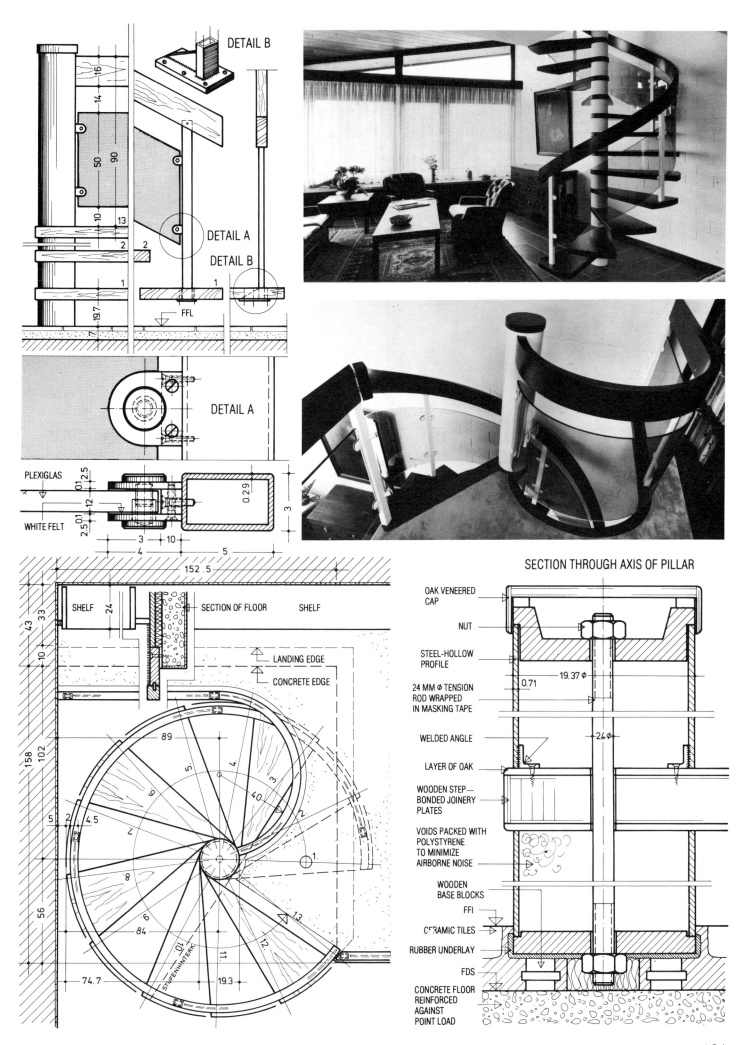

DETAIL B

DETAIL A

DETAIL B

DETAIL A

FFL

PLEXIGLAS

WHITE FELT

SECTION THROUGH AXIS OF PILLAR

SHELF

SECTION OF FLOOR   SHELF

LANDING EDGE

CONCRETE EDGE

STUFENHINTERKA

OAK VENEERED CAP

NUT

STEEL-HOLLOW PROFILE

24 MM Ø TENSION ROD WRAPPED IN MASKING TAPE

WELDED ANGLE

LAYER OF OAK

WOODEN STEP— BONDED JOINERY PLATES

VOIDS PACKED WITH POLYSTYRENE TO MINIMIZE AIRBORNE NOISE

WOODEN BASE BLOCKS

FFI

CERAMIC TILES

RUBBER UNDERLAY

FDS

CONCRETE FLOOR REINFORCED AGAINST POINT LOAD

For this type of stair, it is essential that the wood used should be absolutely dry. It must also be possible to tighten up the tension screws as necessary.

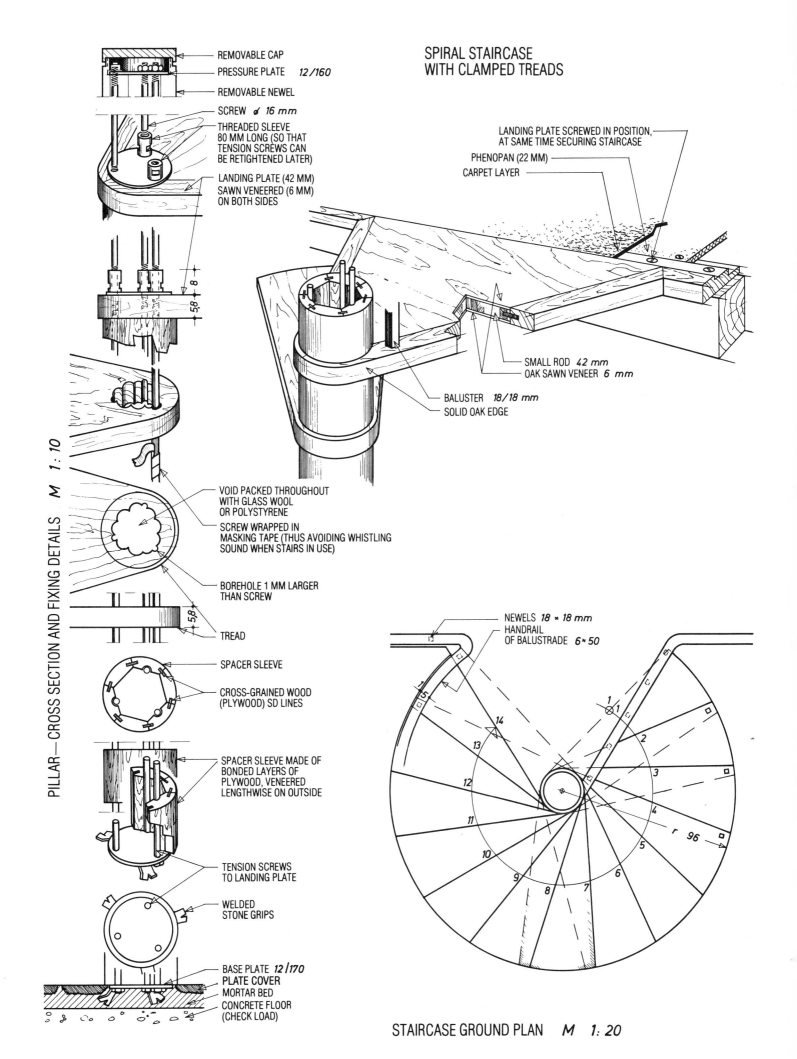

SPIRAL STAIRCASE
WITH CLAMPED TREADS

REMOVABLE CAP
PRESSURE PLATE   12/160
REMOVABLE NEWEL
SCREW ⌀ 16 mm
THREADED SLEEVE
80 MM LONG (SO THAT
TENSION SCREWS CAN
BE RETIGHTENED LATER)
LANDING PLATE (42 MM)
SAWN VENEERED (6 MM)
ON BOTH SIDES

LANDING PLATE SCREWED IN POSITION,
AT SAME TIME SECURING STAIRCASE
PHENOPAN (22 MM)
CARPET LAYER

SMALL ROD   42 mm
OAK SAWN VENEER 6 mm

BALUSTER   18/18 mm
SOLID OAK EDGE

VOID PACKED THROUGHOUT
WITH GLASS WOOL
OR POLYSTYRENE
SCREW WRAPPED IN
MASKING TAPE (THUS AVOIDING WHISTLING
SOUND WHEN STAIRS IN USE)

BOREHOLE 1 MM LARGER
THAN SCREW
TREAD

SPACER SLEEVE
CROSS-GRAINED WOOD
(PLYWOOD) SD LINES

SPACER SLEEVE MADE OF
BONDED LAYERS OF
PLYWOOD, VENEERED
LENGTHWISE ON OUTSIDE

TENSION SCREWS
TO LANDING PLATE
WELDED
STONE GRIPS

BASE PLATE 12/170
PLATE COVER
MORTAR BED
CONCRETE FLOOR
(CHECK LOAD)

PILLAR—CROSS SECTION AND FIXING DETAILS   M 1:10

NEWELS 18 × 18 mm
HANDRAIL
OF BALUSTRADE 6×50

r 96

STAIRCASE GROUND PLAN   M 1:20

The strings and handrails of this solid-mahogany spiral stair are made of bonded laminates. These thin, elegant balusters are constructed in small sections in order to allow the turner to work on them; they are then screwed together.

The same basic construction method has been applied to the three following spiral staircases. The columns of steel tubing are first anchored to the floor with sheet steel brackets which have been welded in position. The treads, which are screwed in place from underneath, rest on the specially angled edges of the sheet steel brackets.

In the sketch (1) a sheet steel bracket is formed for a rectangular sheet; (2 and 3) lengthwise edges are trimmed and the bracket is welded to the steel newel; (4) the tread is screwed to the bracket from beneath; and, in order to prevent the treads from shifting, the gap between the tread and the edges of the steel bracket is filled (5).

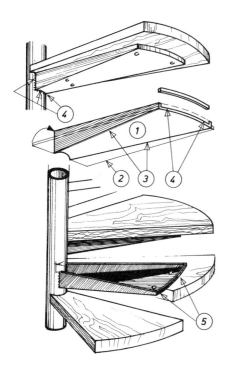

FINISHED STORY HEIGHT 262.5
13 × 20.19   RISE
12 × 21   STEPS

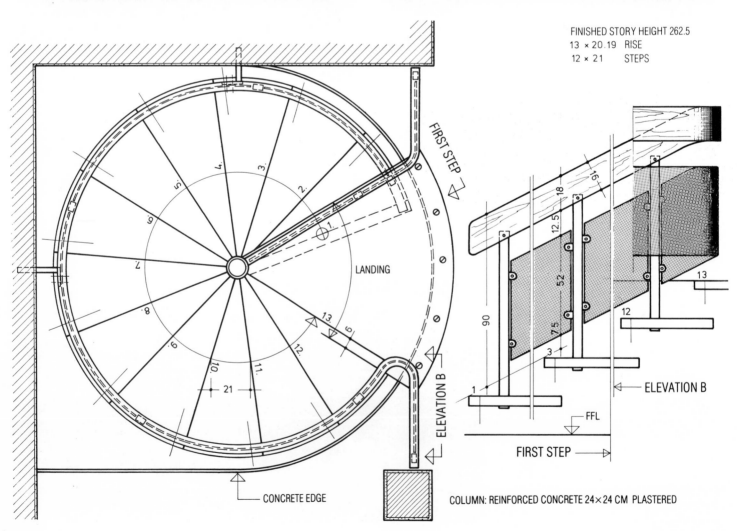

FIRST STEP

LANDING

4.

3.

5.

2.

9.

1.

7.

13.   6

8.

9.

12

10.   11

21

ELEVATION B

ELEVATION B

CONCRETE EDGE

FIRST STEP

COLUMN: REINFORCED CONCRETE 24×24 CM PLASTERED

90   75   52   12.5   18   16

3   12   13

1

FFL

126

The solid welded steel construction of this stair consists of a steel rod, 105 mm in diameter, to which have been welded 3-mm-thick folded sheet steel brackets. The laminated treads are carpeted before they are bolted in position; this deadens their noise in use.

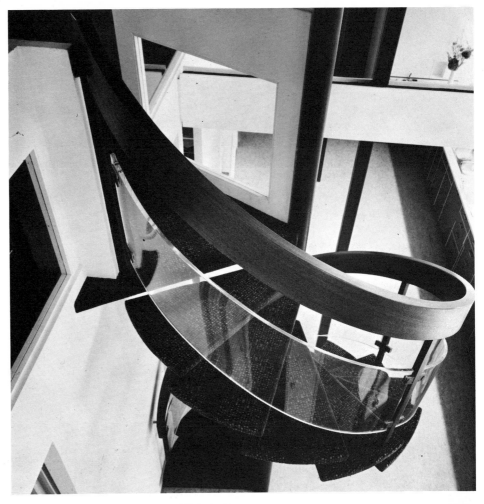

This rustic-style staircase admirably
suits the type of living room in which
it is situated. The top six treads are
suspended from the boards of the
upper parapet. By fixing the landing
slab above firmly in position, the
whole stair is given the stability it
needs.

128

SECTION A—A

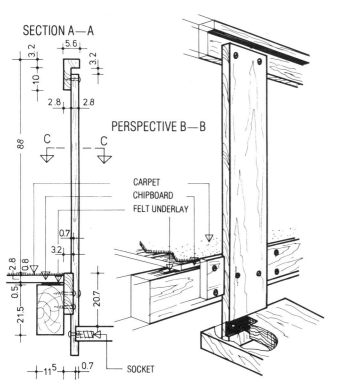

5.6

3.2 3.2

10

2.8 2.8

88

C C

PERSPECTIVE B—B

CARPET
CHIPBOARD
FELT UNDERLAY

0.7

3.2

2.8

0.5 0.8

20.7

21.5

11⁵ 0.7

SOCKET

GROUND PLAN
SECTION C—C

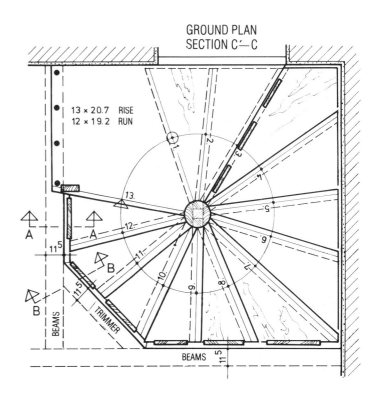

13 × 20.7   RISE
12 × 19.2   RUN

13

12

A A

11⁵

11

10

9

B B

11⁵

BEAMS

TRIMMER

9

8

7

5

1

2

3

4

6

BEAMS

11⁵

The brackets are cantilevered from the central newel and the balusters are screwed in place onto these. The treads are then both bolted and glued to these load-bearing elements. The holes, which carry the hemp rope, have been drilled horizontally in order to create a wave-like effect when the rope is threaded through. The newel, cantilevers, and balusters are oak; the treads are Afzelia.

Using the same basic construction as in the stair on the previous page, the rope is replaced here by a veneered handrail. Note that at the connection of the baseboard with the parquet floor on the landing the surrounding trim is not round as might be expected, but octagonal; this saves a great deal of trouble in rounding off the small parquet sections when the parquet floor is laid.

The spine string in this stair acts as a fixed load-bearing beam. Because of this, the steel supporting standard which has been sunk at the lower end of the string has been anchored to the solid concrete foundations. The balusters above the third step, which are visible in the picture, brace the stair against torsion. Treads, balusters, and handrail are oak, while the laminated timber string is made of pine.

Two offices situated one above the other are connected by this space-saving stair. The staircase enclosure surrounds, which are oak-veneered on both sides, are continued up through the stairwell opening to form a parapet at the upper floor level.

Upper parapet

A steel construction forms the basis for this spiral staircase; its central column has a diameter of 105 mm, the cantilevered treads are made of 3-mm-thick sheet steel, and the material used in the balusters is 8 × 60 mm rolled steel. The handrail is 8 × 60 mm V-2a stainless steel. The sketches below show various other ways in which the balustrade could have been executed.

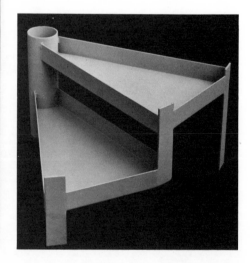

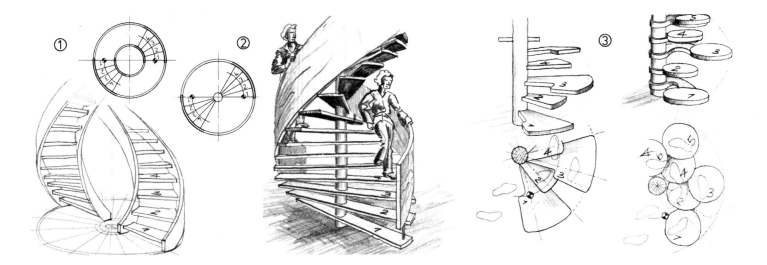

The sketch shows two identical interlocking stairs (1); the idea of one stair leading up, the other down, was the point of departure for this twin-flight spiral stair. Both of the spiral stairs sketched above right (3) are steep and narrow, but they can nevertheless be negotiated with ease because of the way in which the treads are offset. (See also space-saving staircases, page 56.)

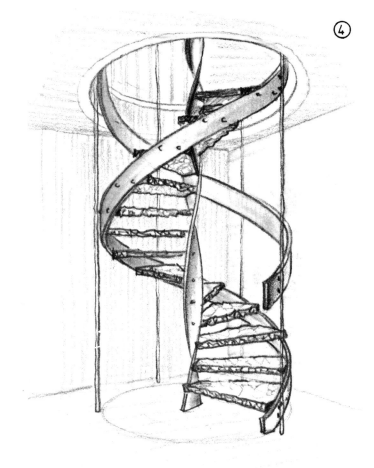

(4) Here, strings, handrail, and newels are produced from approximately ten 160-mm-thick V-2a steel, and the plywood steps, with a depth of 65 mm, are covered with a layer of tufted carpet. The whole staircase is suspended on four steel reinforcing rods and Plexiglas panels can be inserted between the handrail and string. (5) The staircase in this sketch is probably not feasible in practical terms.

135

This decorative spiral staircase, built following the design of the State Architectural Engineering Office in Esslingen, Germany, enhances the entrance hall of a high school. A steel rod serves as the core newel, and this is fastened to a pressure plate and held in position at the top by a triangular steel construction. Each tread is welded individually to the central column and cantilevers outwards without further support, having no connection with the next tread. The balustrade is executed in such a way that it has no connection with the treads and is only connected to the concrete wall at its lower third section. The core of this balustrade, which bears all the loading acting upon it, consists of sections of steel tubing, 50 cm in length, which are welded together when the staircase is assembled. The wooden segments of the balustrade, which are approximately 1 m long, are dovetailed into each other on assembly. They are joined together in such a way as to allow for some subsequent movement and swelling. The expansion joints are packed with a durable plastic filler. The material used is 28-mm raw oak, darkened and sealed.

Both photographs on the right give a size comparison of the staircase and balustrade with the human scale.

The staircase has a "molded" effect when seen from this perspective. The expansion joints between the segments of the balustrade are clearly visible.

The sections of the tread (1) are glued to plates, drilled (2), the groves mortised (3). The balustrade sections are shaped into cones (4), and the tread prepared for bonding and glued into segments (6) on the bonding block (5). A building block (7) determines the direction taken by the core of the spiral. The steel sleeve (8) is seen here on a working model of the tread (9).

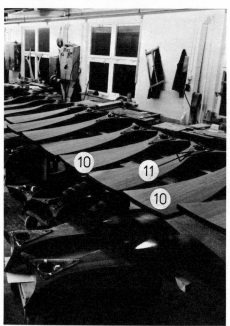

The tread elements (10), fitted with steel sleeves (11), are spread out to dry following the sealing process. The reversed tread (12) shows the surface which has been cut to take the steel sleeve (13). The front edge of the top platform (14) has already been screwed to the head of the spiral (15).

So that every fifth tread (16) can be fitted. the steel construction which will support the top platform (17) is temporarily removed, then subsequently screwed back. The individual treads are very precisely aligned before they are welded to the core newel (18).

The illustration on the far left show the author testing the level of the staircase. On the near left, a steel sleeve is being welded.

138

The base of the balustrade must sustain massive loading. The floorplate is therefore anchored firmly with 24-mm-thick threaded bolts and the surrounding surface area cemented. All the segments are reinforced with a 15 × 15 × 15 mm V welding seam.

These perspectives reveal interesting details of the staircase.

Technical Data:

Story height: 4.46 m
Staircase: External diameter 2.90 m
Balustrade: External diameter 3.40 m
Balustrade length: 15.60 m
Rise: 17.15 cm
Width of going: 27.00 cm
Tubular steel core newel ϕ127/12.5 mm
Tubular steel balustrade segments ϕ 177.8/12.5 mm
Type of wood: darkened oak
Laminae: 22 mm thick

Index of Builders and Architects

Index of Manufacturers

Stair and balustrade combinations were manufactured in the author's workshop. Responsible for assistance in the office: Ch. Bischoff, A. Wagner; in the workshop: E. Tischer; at the point of assembly: F. Rosesprung. Woodwork: W. Mannes Firm, Oberkochen.

Sculpture: H. Sheble, Ellwangen
Turning: G. Liebert, Heidenheim-Schnaitheim
Plastics: Fa. H. Fritz, Heidenheim
　　　　 Fa. W. Mannes, Oberkirchen

Glasswork: Fa. Maier, Heidenheim
　　　　　 Fa. Geiger, Dillingen
Steel girders: Fa. A. Grupp, Oberkochen
　　　　　　 Fa. A. Abele, Oberkochen
　　　　　　 Fa. J. A. Bauerle, Oberkochen-Essingen

Photographers: R. Werner, K. Werner. U. Furwangler

Index